A GIFT
from
BRITTANY

A GIFT

from

BRITTANY

A MEMOIR OF LOVE AND LOSS
IN THE
FRENCH COUNTRYSIDE

MARJORIE PRICE

GOTHAM BOOKS

Some names and identifying characteristics have been changed to protect the privacy of the individuals involved.

GOTHAM BOOKS
Published by Penguin Group (USA) Inc.
375 Hudson Street, New York, New York 10014, U.S.A.
Penguin Group (Canada), 90 Eglinton Avenue East, Suite 700, Toronto, Ontario M4P 2Y3, Canada (a division of Pearson Penguin Canada Inc.); Penguin Books Ltd, 80 Strand, London WC2R 0RL, England; Penguin Ireland, 25 St Stephen's Green, Dublin 2, Ireland (a division of Penguin Books Ltd); Penguin Group (Australia), 250 Camberwell Road, Camberwell, Victoria 3124, Australia (a division of Pearson Australia Group Pty Ltd); Penguin Books India Pvt Ltd, 11 Community Centre, Panchsheel Park, New Delhi—110 017, India; Penguin Group (NZ), 67 Apollo Drive, Rosedale, North Shore 0632, New Zealand (a division of Pearson New Zealand Ltd); Penguin Books (South Africa) (Pty) Ltd, 24 Sturdee Avenue, Rosebank, Johannesburg 2196, South Africa

Penguin Books Ltd, Registered Offices: 80 Strand, London WC2R 0RL, England

Published by Gotham Books, a member of Penguin Group (USA) Inc.

First printing, April 2008
10 9 8 7 6 5 4 3 2 1

Gotham Books and the skyscraper logo are trademarks of Penguin Group (USA) Inc.

LIBRARY OF CONGRESS CATALOGING-IN-PUBLICATION DATA HAS BEEN APPLIED FOR.

ISBN 978-1-592-40350-9

Printed in the United States of America
Set in Sabon • *Designed by Elke Sigal*

While the author has made every effort to provide accurate telephone numbers and Internet addresses at the time of publication, neither the publisher nor the author assumes any responsibility for errors, or for changes that occur after publication. Further, the publisher does not have any control over and does not assume any responsibility for author or third-party Web sites or their content.

To Jeanne

Prologue

⌒

THE VILLAGE DOESN'T EXIST ANYMORE. Outwardly it appears the same until you notice the gleaming, prefabricated buildings sprinkled among age-old farmhouses. The villagers aren't there, either. No longer do you see them trudging off to fields long before daylight has broken through the mist. The sight of old peasant women in long black skirts, bent over cabbages in their vegetable gardens, has vanished, along with that of peasants clustered around a fence, chattering among themselves in patois, indivisible from their ancient surroundings. Except on postcards for tourists, the sight of women pinning on their stiff lace coifs, their black skirts billowing in the wind, scurrying across a meadow to attend Sunday Mass in a nearby village, is long forgotten. The custom of huddling around a fireplace at one of the farmhouses on dark, wintry nights to keep warm, drink cider, and tell ghost stories to pass the time is no more. A way of life that endured for centuries is gone.

But years ago, when I was young, I found myself there,

among them. At first, the village and the people who lived there were unfamiliar and forbidding to me. Then, in time, I grew close to one of them—to Jeanne—and the village became my world, too.

In an old hand-carved wooden chest, I keep a memento that I have treasured for nearly fifty years. It is a coif, the kind of cap the women used to wear on Sundays or whenever they ventured from their farms and villages. No longer white, tinged with gray from age, it is wrapped in tissue paper and pressed flat like petals of a flower enfolded between pages of a book. It is no ordinary coif; it is a special kind worn only for feasts and weddings. The center is made of netting, and all around is lace, thickly starched yet delicate. As I hold it in my hand, distant memories flood across my mind, memories of love and heartbreak, and of a simple peasant woman dressed in black who transformed my life.

My fingers run along the highs and crevices of the lace, remembering the day she pinned it on me. How vividly the memory of that day sharpens into focus; she is by my side, and the village comes to life again.

1

Pounded Dirt

For a long time driving back to Paris, I stared out of the car window, transfixed by skeletal branches illuminated by our headlights and silhouetted against starless skies. Speeding through the wintry Breton landscape, neither of us spoke. Yves kept his eyes fixed on the road ahead. At last, he broke the silence.

"Think of it, Midge, seven houses and three hectares. We'll own half of a hamlet!"

I said nothing, which might have been interpreted as sulking.

"Come on," he coaxed. "You have to admit for that many houses and all those trees, sixty-seven million francs is an unbelievable bargain."

"A bargain? For seven broken-down farmhouses? I can't believe you'd even think of buying the place."

Unfazed, he rhapsodized about how sturdy the houses were, how the pinewoods in back spread out for miles, and what a great find it was. "Just imagine. We'll have our very own forest."

I turned to him. "Yves," I implored, "have you forgotten? We wanted a cozy farmhouse by the sea where we could paint beautiful pictures. Not an oversized wreck buried off in the woods. This place is so run-down we'd spend the next twenty years fixing it up!"

"Listen, Mijoux," he said. There it was: the name he called me when he was being affectionate, apologetic, or persuasive. "With all that space, we'll both have plenty of room to paint." Besides, he went on, he would build a studio in the woods behind the main house, off by himself and private, the kind he had always wanted. And I could fix up one of the empty buildings as my very own studio.

"Which one?" I replied icily. "They're all in ruin."

"They just look that way on the outside, *chérie*. But they're solid. Look, I know the place is bigger than what we were looking for, but we only need to restore the houses we'll live in. And next spring, while we wait for the Blevenecs to finish their new farm, we'll move into the one by the road, and—"

"Next to the *cows*?" I slammed my fist down on the dashboard so hard the glove compartment sprang open. "Absolutely not!" I meant it. No one could get me to live in that dismal shack next to the stable that had harbored spiderwebs and rats' nests for the past hundred years. No one, not even Yves, could persuade me.

"We'll fix it up," he said. A muscular arm reached out and drew me to him. "The house already has a working fireplace. All we need is a double-burner camper's stove for cooking, a mattress on the floor for us, and a bed for Danielle. The Blevenecs' youngest is only two years older than she is. She'll have someone to play with. Think how robust she'll become, spending summer months away from the city, breathing fresh country air. You'll see, *ma chérie*. La Salle is just what we've been looking for."

⌒

From the time I met Yves, that first amorous spring of 1960, he used to tell me about the farmhouse he would buy one day in the French countryside. It would be a refuge from Paris summers, a hideaway surrounded by nature where he would paint, far removed from distractions of the big city. After we married and Danielle was born, we daydreamed about what the house would be like and where we would find it. Yves' first choice was Auvergne, the central mountainous region of France where he had spent childhood summers, but Auvergne was a full day's drive from Paris; we needed something closer. My fantasy had always been to live near the sea in the South of France, with its mimosa-perfumed air and sun-drenched cities along the Mediterranean. Yves insisted that the Midi had been despoiled by tourists, and besides, the South was even farther from Paris than Auvergne. The Midi was out.

Gradually our search whittled down to Brittany. La Bretagne. Surrounded on three sides by sea, Brittany was primitive, unspoiled, had a Celtic soul to satisfy and inspire Yves, and I quickly adjusted to the prospect of a homey farmhouse along a rocky coastline. A mere six hours from Paris, Brittany would be close enough for either of us to rush back on short notice to see a gallery dealer or art collector. At last we knew what we wanted.

With Yves' coaching, I wrote my father, asking him for a loan for a small farmhouse in the country to spend our summers and promised we would pay him back as soon as possible. "Danielle will breathe fresh, healthy air," I wrote, "and surrounded by nature, Yves and I will produce paintings that surely will lead to success in the art world." He wrote back saying, "I hope you're right, my dear. Your head has always been in the clouds, but I am sending you the money as a belated wedding present, anyway." We were overjoyed. All we needed now was luck in finding the right place. We contacted *notaires* throughout Brittany: those omnipresent creatures in France who handle every transaction from birth to death to inheritance and purchases of property.

One day, after countless disappointing leads, a *notaire* from the south of Brittany telephoned us in Paris.

"I have found it!" Maître Rowan bellowed into the phone. "*Quelle chance!* It is exactly the place for you! *La moitié d'un hameau.* Imagine! Half of a hamlet. *Mon dieu*, only twelve kilometers from the enchanting town of Vannes. Perhaps somewhat larger than what you had in mind. *Eh, oui*, instead of one farmhouse, you will have seven. Otherwise, the place is perfect. *Parfait!* Besides, the price is negotiable. Have confidence in me," he effused. "This one you must see."

Yves slammed down the phone. "Merde! He must be kidding. Half a hamlet!"

"What's a hamlet?" I asked.

"A small village! He's completely crazy."

He twirled a finger against his forehead and stormed back to his studio. Moments later, the door flew open. "I've changed my mind," he said. "I'm going to take a look. At least we'll have an idea of what's available in the region." The following

6

morning, he drove off in our tiny Deux Chevaux for the southern part of Brittany called the Morbihan, and that evening, he telephoned. "The *notaire* was right, *chérie*. You have to see it for yourself. Never mind that it's big. Drop Danielle off at my parents' house. Take the six-thirty train tomorrow morning that gets to Vannes at half past noon. I'll be waiting for you at the station. We'll drive out to see it. It's called La Salle."

The next day, I arrived at a quaint, immaculate red brick railway station at the edge of town. Yves waved at me from a nearly deserted platform, I rushed into his outstretched arms, and we were on our way. After a short ride along the highway, he turned onto a narrow, winding country road. "The hamlet is only twelve kilometers from Vannes," Yves said. "It's the place we've been dreaming about. You're going to love it, Mijoux. I know you will."

"Uh-huh." Despite his enthusiasm, I was far from enamored with the landscape. For one thing, we were heading inland. I had been drawn to Brittany for its rugged shoreline and had counted on being near the sea. What's more, there was no sign of anyone; not a single car passed us along the road. Trying to ignore a sinking feeling in the pit of my stomach, I reassured myself we were just looking and settled back to admire the scenery, which, in spite of myself, I had to admit was peaceful and unspoiled. Bounded by thick hedges, interspersed with mysterious paths branching off and leading seemingly to nowhere, the serpentine road meandered endlessly with no apparent destination in sight. A few farmhouses, barely visible, emerged here and there in the distance. All around, the landscape was lush, while not as rugged and wild as what I had seen from the train, reinforcing Yves' assurance that the south of Brittany had a mild and occasionally sunny climate. Struggling to pronounce strange-sounding names carved on makeshift signs along the road, I read aloud, "Locqueltas, Kerlomen, Keravello . . . Le Guerhuet. What language is that?" I said. "Are we still in France?"

"That's Breton," Yves explained. "In most of Brittany, the language was, and in places still is, Breton. But in the Morbihan, near Vannes, they speak Gallo, a mixture of patois, Breton, and French words like La Salle. It used to be the only language spoken here. Then the government passed a law, forbidding people to speak it. They actually put up signs saying NO SPITTING OR SPEAKING BRETON, and that included Gallo. After the war, the law was revoked. But even today, speaking Breton or Gallo isn't allowed in schools. Still, they can't stop the older peasants from speaking these dying languages among themselves."

I smiled smugly to myself. If only my friends in Chicago could see me, they wouldn't believe their eyes. I was supposed to be living a carbon copy of their lives, married to a steady, reliable Midwesterner—someone like my old boyfriend Charlie—and settled down in the suburbs. Instead, here I was, married to an exciting French painter, with an adorable French-speaking two-and-a-half-year-old daughter, and off on an adventure to find an idyllic farmhouse in the French countryside where we would spend our summers. I could hardly believe it myself.

The road continued endlessly. Twelve kilometers felt more like thirty as one unannounced curve followed another and our city-bred Deux Chevaux bounced and vaulted over the unpaved, bumpy road. How rural can this place be? I wondered.

"Here we are," he exclaimed. "That's La Salle!"

"Where?"

"There!"

We turned onto a dirt road that climbed a sloping hill. From the car window, all I could see was an ugly stone and cement wall that dominated the horizon like an ill-boding fortress bulging through ramparts and spilling over the hillside. We drove on. Moments later a pine forest that spread across the crest of the hill came into view, shading clusters of farmhouses to the right and to the left of the road. Yves swung left onto a dirt courtyard. I gasped. Fifty feet before us loomed a huge, dilapidated farmhouse. To the right were several more; another stretched across the courtyard and was bigger than any edifice I had ever seen before; and near the entrance were another two. I shuddered to think how many more might materialize as the day progressed. Extricating myself from the Deux Chevaux, I came face-to-face with the front of the block-long apparition I had seen from below. Upon closer inspection, it proved to be an enormous storehouse, overflowing with broken wagons, discarded wheelbarrows, retired plows, tools, castaway hoes, rusted rakes, spades, and junk. Heaving and rattling in the wind like the hulk of an old, dying elephant, it dwarfed the other buildings and cast a mammoth shadow over the courtyard, accentuating the feeling of desolation that permeated the place. I followed Yves, tiptoeing cautiously to avoid tin cans, scraps of discarded tools, and unidentifiable animal droppings. Sidestepping an extended family of chickens, we passed in front of the farmhouses, which were marginally more pleasing than the oversize eyesore at the entrance. All the buildings had meter-thick stone walls and dark gray slate roofs, and were in various stages of disrepair. Slabs of aluminum lay helter-skelter over missing tiles on the roofs. Ill-fitting pieces of wood boarded up windows, their original stone frames replaced by unsightly patches of cement. This was the country house of our dreams? Certainly he couldn't be contemplating buying such a monstrosity. Nothing could have been further removed from the picturesque Breton farmhouse of Gauguin paintings I assumed we were looking for. This was *The Grapes of Wrath.*

I wrinkled my nose in disgust, but Yves paid no attention. He was nodding to a couple advancing single-mindedly in our direction. Everyone shook hands and smiled when I remembered Yves had told me not to speak, since if anyone found out I was American, they might double the price. Although what possible difference would that make, I thought, since we certainly would never buy the place!

In his late thirties, the man was tall, held himself stiffly, and had well-defined, handsome features. His wife, by contrast, was plump, ruddy-complexioned, and giggled like a young girl. It occurred to me that talking to strangers was not a part of her life, whereas I loved talking to strangers, especially those whose lives were different from mine. Walking alongside her, I longed to ask what it was like living on an isolated farm far off in the country. I wanted to know where she did her shopping and was she an only child? How many children did she have, and what she was cooking for supper? The more I thought about not being able to speak, the more insatiable became my curiosity and the more shackled I felt by the no-talking edict.

Her face flushed, Madame Blevenec invited us into the main farmhouse. The large, rectangular room served as both kitchen and living space, with bunk beds lined alongside the walls for her and her husband and their five children, as well as her frail, bent-over father, who shuffled in and out of the kitchen, eyeing us suspiciously as Yves and Monsieur Blevenec spoke. From a corner of the dark room drifted the unmistakable smell of cabbage soup simmering on a wood-burning stove. Beams of light from two narrow windows pierced the gloom, and one bare lightbulb dangled by a twisted wire from a rafter next to a coiled, sticky paper that had succeeded in luring and ensnaring flies. Millions of them. I was soon to learn that where there are cows, there are flies—fat, rubbery, voracious, indestructible flies.

Madame Blevenec brought four glasses from the cupboard, wiped each one with her apron, and placed them on a wooden table along with a loaf of bread, a tin box of cookies, and a chunk of lard. We took our places on benches along each side of the table. Monsieur Blevenec pulled a knife from his overalls; his wife took a knife from a pocket in her apron and, observing that we didn't come equipped with our own, handed knives to Yves and me. There was minimal conversation. Monsieur Blevenec opened a bottle of homemade cider, and to my astonishment, the men lunged into a discussion of a possible sale.

"*Alors*, Monsieur Drumont, you saw the plot of land at the bottom of the hill," said Monsieur Blevenec, leaning forward, his eyes gleaming. "It's there we'll lay the foundation for our new house." He cut a thick slice of bread, spread it with lard, and handed it to me. "And next year, we're going to buy a tractor. In the whole village, *dame*, ours will be the first and only one."

Everyone ate and drank. It was my introduction to cider and lard. The lard reminded me of the slippery texture of raw oysters with the consistency of a gummy gel medium I use to mix my paints. The cider smelled and tasted like a mixture of stale vinegar and turpentine. I choked everything down as discreetly as possible.

"La Sallette," blurted Mrs. Blevenec, reddening and turning toward her husband for approval. "We're calling our new house La Sallette." It was her first contribution to the conversation, far more than I had been allowed to make. The Blevenecs must have thought I was shy, severely retarded, or had no opinion. How wrong they were; I was dying to speak. Deciding on a place in the country was crucial and this was the last place in the world where I would ever agree to spend half of the rest of my life, although a thick piece of lard had glued itself to the roof of my mouth, leaving me no choice but to keep silent.

"Next spring, you and your wife can move into the first farmhouse, the one to the right as you enter the courtyard. We can take a look." Monsieur Blevenec pushed his bench away from the table and stood up. Yves did the same and motioned for me to join them. Madame Blevenec remained in the kitchen.

"*Vous voyez,* Monsieur and Madame Drumont," Monsieur Blevenec explained as we crossed the courtyard, "this side of the village was once divided into two farms. The house next to the road and the one where you would be staying are the oldest in the hamlet. See how the stones were cut and chipped so they dovetail without anything holding them together?" He slid his thumb along the edge of one of the stones. "In this part of the farm, the houses are at least three hundred years old."

"Then your house is more recent," Yves said, "because the stones are joined with cement?"

"Right. But two hundred years is still plenty old. Isn't that so, Madame Drumont?" He smiled. I smiled back and out of habit, started to answer him as Yves stepped quickly between us. Monsieur Blevenec yanked open the door and motioned for me to enter. Inside was dark and musty. From an overhead rafter swung the ever-present naked bulb, and the floor was the usual *terre battue*. Pounded dirt. Did people actually live on solid packed earth? For decades the house had been abandoned, another nightmarish, albeit smaller, depository of junk. Worst of all, it was at a right angle to the stable where the cows were kept. Would I ever agree to live in such close proximity to cows? Of course not! A temporary house? Preposterous. Still, I didn't need to be overly concerned. Oh, God, I hoped not. We *were* only looking, weren't we?

Returning to the kitchen, we rejoined Madame Blevenec, who had set out cups and was pouring a strong, bitter-smelling coffee laced with chicory root, as I later learned was the custom in the country. We resumed our places on the wooden benches.

"When you consider there are seven houses and three hectares in the bargain, Monsieur Drumont, seventy-two million francs isn't a high price."

I whipped around to face Yves.

"But we would have huge expenses repairing the roofs, installing heating, modernizing, insulating. It's too big a job, Monsieur Blevenec. Sixty-five million," said Yves.

"Sixty-nine million," countered Monsieur Blevenec. "I can't go any lower, Monsieur Drumont."

There was a pause. I held my breath. "We'll need to think about it," Yves said. I exhaled and made a motion to get up and leave.

"Sixty-seven million." Yves said, "That is our final offer, Monsieur Blevenec."

Monsieur Blevenec tipped back his bench. His wife stood and signaled for him to join her. "We'll be right back," he said, and they left the room.

"I'll bet they're talking over our offer," Yves whispered close to my ear as if we were co-conspirators.

"*Our* offer! You haven't even asked my opinion!"

"Shhh. They'll hear you. Listen, *chérie*," he said, pulling me to my feet and putting his hands on my shoulders, "I know this place doesn't look like much from the outside. But you don't know the French countryside as I do. You don't know these villages or these old farmhouses. I've known them since I was a child and I can see the possibilities. La Salle is going to be fabulous once we fix it up. Trust me."

"Yves," I said in a husky voice, "we can't buy this place. It's too big. It's too *old*. The floors are dirt! You know what that means? Dirt floors!" My voice sounded desperate, as though I had dropped to my knees and was pleading with him. "Have you forgotten, *chéri*? We wanted a little farmhouse by the sea, where we could paint. If we bought this ruin, we'd be too busy picking up the rubble. Not only that . . ."

He went on as if he hadn't heard a word. "Believe me, Midge. This place is perfect. It's an incredible buy for the money. Dad will say we made a great investment."

"But, but . . ." I stammered.

Too late. They were back.

When the Blevenecs sat down again, they were business-like and formal. Considering the timing of their private conference, I wondered if Mrs. Blevenec might be the one who made financial decisions behind closed doors, or at the very least, was consulted before they were carved in stone, unlike the hierarchical procedure that ruled in my family.

"*D'accord,*" Monsieur Blevenec began slowly. "Sixty-seven million. I accept."

They shook hands. Monsieur Blevenec brought another bottle of cider to the table. They drank, loosened up, laughed together, and agreed that the first payment would be made as soon as the official papers had been signed. Sipping my cider in silence, I found it less offensive with each swallow. Numbly, I decided I might as well get drunk.

"My wife is from Chicago," Yves announced, acknowledging my presence now that the price was settled and danger had passed. All eyes shifted to me.

"*Oui, je suis de* Chicago," I said, clearing my throat.

"But you speak French! Maître Rowan told us you are American," said Monsieur Blevenec. "We thought you spoke only American."

I glared at Yves.

"Chicago is a dangerous place, *non?*" asked Monsieur Blevenec.

"Not since the days of Al Capone," I said.

"This is the first time an American ever set foot at La Salle. You'll be welcome here, *dame.*" He reached across the table to shake my hand.

"*Dame, oui!*" said Mrs. Blevenec with a shy smile, blushing, and nodding in agreement.

⌒

Everyone shook hands, and we said goodbye. It was then, as we piled into the Deux Chevaux and began driving out of the courtyard, that I saw her. She was standing by the side of the road, an old peasant woman dressed in black, bent over from working in the fields, and wrinkled and worn from the sun and wind. What struck me most was the aura of timelessness about her, as if she had stepped out of another century. I rolled down a frost-covered window to get a better glimpse of her. Her hair was drawn back into a bun. A woolen scarf tied under her chin flapped against her cheek as an icy gust whipped across the country road. She leaned toward the car, and it startled me when our eyes met. I kept staring back at her as we turned to drive down the hill. Her long black skirt billowed in the January wind, but she stood as motionless as one of those mysterious, towering stone menhirs that emerge from parts of the Breton landscape. How alien she was to the twentieth century; how seamlessly she blended in with the ancient setting. Brushed by wintry shadows and silhouetted against the age-old village, she was inseparable from the stone and slate farmhouses rising from the ground behind her.

What in the world was I doing here? I asked myself. I could never live in such a forlorn and isolated village. And these strange people whom I could hardly understand, I could never live among them.

And yet, I couldn't put her out of my mind. Her name, I learned later, was Jeanne Montrelay. Her image lingered in my mind all the way to Paris. As the last echoes of wintry sunlight sank beneath the horizon, I kept seeing her face, wrinkled and round like the sun, intermingling like an ever-changing kaleidoscope with the darkening French countryside racing behind us.

2

Twists of Fate

FOUR YEARS EARLIER, IN AN UPSCALE tree-lined suburb of Chicago along the shores of Lake Michigan, I had just turned twenty-eight. After college, I found work as a secretary in television and attended art school at night. For as long as I could remember, I had dreamed of going to Paris to paint. Everything French enthralled me. I read all I could unearth about France and French artists. I struggled through French language classes, devoured French food, and made mayonnaise by dripping salad oil drop by drop into egg yolk and mustard as I was sure any respectable French housewife would do. By living at home and rationing myself to a twenty-cent hot dog every day for lunch, I saved enough money to buy a third-class ticket to France on the *Queen Elizabeth*. If I were frugal enough, I calculated, I could stay for three months.

It was 1960. Most young women in their twenties were concentrating on getting married. And during the early sixties, most Americans who ventured to Europe were rich families, traveling first class with governesses for the children and countless steamer trunks filled with sequined evening clothes for sumptuous dinners at the captain's table. Third class, on the other hand, was crammed with immigrant families sailing back to the old country and an occasional pair of adventurous schoolteachers on summer vacation. Rarely did anyone go alone, especially young women. Not surprisingly, my family was scandalized at the thought of my traveling to France by myself.

"I won't hear of it!" growled my businessman father, coming out from behind the *Chicago Tribune*. He and I had always been close. While I was growing up, we used to take long walks together along Lake Michigan on Sunday mornings and stop to chat with fishermen standing on the piers jutting out into the lake. He was a champion swimmer and taught me to love swimming when I was a tot. "You wrap him around your little finger," my mother used to say. I adored him and hated to displease him. But sometimes it couldn't be helped.

"Well-brought-up young women do not travel alone, especially not to France," my mother said in a tremulous voice and on the verge of tears. "Everyone keeps asking when you're going to settle down and get married. If you go off to Europe by yourself, what will I tell my friends?" I tried to reassure her, but what people thought was of vital concern to her. She had raised me to behave like a lady: pearls and white gloves were de rigueur, and any minor deviation was unthinkable. As far as she was concerned, traveling on my own to Europe was tantamount to sin.

"At least you might have the decency to sign up with a tour, like *I* did after my graduation," taunted my older sister, hardly neutralizing the situation. "Of course," she added, "we stayed at the Hôtel Crillon—the only decent place to stay in Paris."

Any hope of encouragement from my boyfriend, Charlie, was soon squelched. Charlie and I had been "going together" for nearly a year. Neither of us was impatient to marry; we just assumed that in time we would end up together. He was an announcer at the television station where I worked. Tall, with strong, photogenic features, he had a deep, sonorous voice that made everything he said sound profound. He smoked a pipe, which reminded me of my father, and was charming to a fault with my mother. While not the most exciting man I had ever imagined, he was reliable and devoted. Besides, when I met him, I was fed up with dating and warding off unwanted advances. Charlie was different. He proclaimed his respect for me, sent me flowers after every date, and assured me that our relationship would remain chaste until "the right time." I convinced myself that when that time came, I would fall in love. However, when I told him of my intention to go to France for several months, his imperturbable nature erupted into a rare display of rage. During a tense and near-final dinner date at our favorite Chinese restaurant, he waved his arms and shouted, "No fiancée of mine is going to a foreign country overrun with Latin lovers!"

Still, I was determined. I knew if I wanted to be an artist, I had to have this experience. I had to leave home and friends far behind, if only for a few months. Neither my family nor Charlie could possibly understand the depth of my drive, my passion for art. I had my ticket and a small bank account, and I would let nothing stand in my way. Accompanied by a barrage of scoldings and ultimatums, I packed two small suitcases, took the train to New York City, boarded the ship, and never looked back.

Once in Paris, I felt free and indestructible, as if I were rushing into unknown waters where anything was possible. The noisy, exuberant city was a dizzying contrast to the bland, homogeneous Chicago suburb I had left behind. Everything enchanted me. Walking along the Seine brought to life the Impressionist paintings I loved so much. I couldn't believe I was actually seeing the same lustrous city that had inspired all those dauntless painters one hundred years ago. Day after day, I explored the narrow, winding streets of the city. I couldn't believe I was walking through the same streets with their nuances of grays and sunlight burning through the fog that Pissarro and Sisley and all the others had immortalized and whose paintings I knew by heart. I filled sketchbook after sketchbook with spires of the Notre Dame cathedral, Rodin statues, wrought-iron balconies, courtyards, policemen, lovers along the Seine, everything in sight. Sketching people in cafés along the boulevards was my tireless pursuit. I would ease into a curbside table and order a café crème as nonchalantly as possible. The faces of people chattering unintelligibly nearby looked different to me from American faces. Their features were sharper, their noses more pointed and narrower, their mouths pinched and birdlike, undoubtedly from all the stretching and puckering required to pronounce those elusive French sounds.

I made the rounds of art shows. In an elegant gallery on the Right Bank, a distinguished-looking, suave director approached me and inquired if I liked the exhibition. In spite of my minimal French vocabulary, I managed to say, *"Est-ce que je dois être,* uh, *honnête?"*

"*Bien sûr*, mademoiselle, one must always be honest," he replied with unmistakable Gallic charm.

The truth was I didn't like the paintings at all. They were figurative, but kowtowing to the current favor of abstraction, they were roughly executed with a palette knife. "The work looks, uh, *facile*," I said, tactfully avoiding the word *commercial*.

"I see what you mean, mademoiselle. Hmm . . . *Mais oui. Facile*." He stroked his silvery hair. "But if you are interested in seeing the work of another painter, I will send you an invitation to the vernissage next week of a young and talented artist named Le Guerrec. Perhaps he will be more to your liking."

⌒

The opening for Le Guerrec was under way when I arrived. The gallery was packed with sophisticated and eccentric-looking people milling about and gesturing to one another from across the room. Thrilled to be at my first Parisian art opening, I was devouring the scene when suddenly everyone and everything in the crowded gallery slipped out of focus with the exception of a man who stood out as distinctly as if a phosphorescent spotlight were shining on him in a blacked-out theater. Startlingly good-looking and in his thirties, he had a classic Roman profile, an asymmetric, prominent nose, and a thin, sensuous mouth. Broad shouldered and muscular, he was taller than most Frenchmen. He dressed with a casual flair and wore an open shirt with a chic red and black paisley foulard at his neck. He exuded confidence, a kind of natural superiority as he gazed over the heads of people crowding through the rooms of the exhibition.

Since he appeared to be the epitome of a French artist, I assumed at first that he was the painter. But he remained by the side of a gaunt young man with long black hair and a high voice, wearing a rumpled floor-length ebony velvet cape and who, on closer observation, proved to be the creator of the paintings. The two men joked together and obviously were friends.

I circled around the gallery in slow motion several times, brushing past the two of them, ostensibly intent on examining art. They didn't even notice me. In the vestibule, I collected my coat and was about to leave when the tall one materialized at the gallery door, blocking my exit.

"Does it interest you to have your portrait painted?" he said, with a caressing look that made me feel weak in the knees.

"*Oui!*" I blurted and scribbled my name and the telephone number of my hotel on a scrap of paper. "Please call," I murmured in my best French, slipping the note into his surprised, outstretched hand.

A week later, he called. "*Allo,* Midge," he said, pronouncing my name with a French accent and transforming it into a silken sounding "Mee-je." It had never sounded like that before. "*C'est Yves.* We met at Le Guerrec's vernissage. Do you remember me?"

"I think so. 'Yves.' Oh, yes, of course, the exhibition," I tossed out in my most devil-may-care manner.

"Listen, it would please me if you would come to my studio on Friday evening for dinner and to see my paintings. A group of English collectors are coming as well. Can you join us?"

Somehow I waited until Friday. I arrived punctually at eight. Inexplicably, the English collectors never showed up.

In his small, sparsely equipped kitchen, he prepared dinner, and although my French was limited, he seemed to be the most intelligent man I had ever met. He was articulate, poetic, and had studied Greek and Latin as well as French, English, and my own American literary classics. Dinner, however, was not haute cuisine. It consisted of overcooked and underseasoned stove-top grilled beefsteak, served with a tasteless, soggy, inedible rice, thankfully washed down with a pleasant red wine.

After dinner, we went into the studio to look at paintings. Spacious and cluttered at the same time, it was exactly as I had always imagined a French artist's studio to be. One entire wall consisted of windows with northern light, and along a high ceiling were gnarled wooden rafters. Over a sagging sofa, sturdy beams supported a platform on which paintings were stored, leaning against one another like worn and familiar books on a shelf. A long wooden table stretched along one side of the studio on which countless tubes and jars of paint, at once orderly and haphazard, were lined up side by side. Brushes of all kinds and shapes and palette knives were crammed into oversize tin cans. Paintings leaned against the walls everywhere, some presumably done, some in progress.

Abstract Expressionism was in its heyday in the early sixties. At the art school I had gone to, representational art was considered *dépassé* and frowned upon. Yves' work was defiantly realistic. All his subject matter was inspired by nature. Some paintings were of flowers—not static, traditional still lifes, but nameless flowers that spilled out of the canvas in effusions of reds, whites, or yellows. Sometimes his palette was in tones of blue, and those paintings were melancholic. Others were in shades of ocher, with yellows, rusts, browns, and umbers interweaving on the canvas, making a sun-drenched field shimmer and glisten. Some paintings were of birds: owls, crows, and turkeys; while realistic, they were prototypes, mythical and haunting. He set a painting he had just finished of a pheasant on the easel. Painted with bursts of reds, browns, oranges, and olive greens, the pheasant stood against a lush background, as if a field had come alive and the bird had sprung from it. It was the most exquisite painting I had ever seen. In all Yves' work, the paint was thick and tactile, without detectable signs of brushwork or palette knife. It was as if paint had fallen by its own power onto the canvas without calculation or design and had magically twisted and intertwined to become these objects of beauty. I was transfixed. Yves sat next to me on the sofa. I searched for words to describe how I felt about his work. It would have been hard to find adequate words in English, let alone in French. One by one, his paintings had enveloped me and transported me to a place I had never been before. As I spoke, I felt an arm sliding surreptitiously around my waist.

"I am pleased you like my work," he said softly, drawing me to him and moving in closer.

"Like it! These are the most extraordinary paintings I've ever seen. They are so powerful. I never expected . . ."

He leaned over to kiss me. It was a long, tender, unforgettable kiss. It didn't occur to me to protest. We kissed again. Then without further ado, he stood up, took me by the arm, and began to lead me, dazed, toward the bedroom, which was in the back of the apartment. Reality seeped through the haze. The trance was broken. I had always thought of myself as worldly, not easily ruffled in situations like this. But instead of remaining cool and sophisticated, I began to cry. Without warning, uncontrollably. Through sobs I heard myself say in a girlish voice, "You're just like all the others!" Distraught, I pulled away, grabbed my coat, and without waiting for the elevator, ran down six flights of stairs and into the street.

That was the first night. He called at my hotel the next day, apologized for his boorish behavior, and suggested I come over that evening. I went back to his studio, cooked dinner, and then, as though predetermined, we made love. Although it was the first time, it seemed we had been together forever, as if our bodies belonged to each other. I lost all sense of time and place, past and future; all that mattered was that very moment, being there with him. I never knew I could be so powerfully drawn to someone. He was the most beautiful and sensuous man I had ever known. But it was much more than that. It was everything about him. How attentive he was to everything I said, even when I struggled to find the right word in French. How he called me his sorceress. How he turned down the lights and lit candles to read poems he had written, and even some he had dedicated to me. How much his paintings moved me. How the thought of being with a French artist thrilled me. How we discussed art for hours, and how his ideas illuminated me and made me believe I would become the artist I had dreamed of being. How I felt more deeply loved by him than by anyone else in my life, and how, when enclosed in his arms, I knew I had found the one man I would always love.

From then on, he was the only man I cared to see. It had never been my intention to remain permanently in France. I always assumed I would return to Chicago when my money ran out, get a job, and end up marrying Charlie, if he would still have me. Dear, patient Charlie. His weekly letters arrived at my hotel without fail. They were warm, newsy, and irrelevant to my new life. By the summer, I was spending nearly every night at Yves' apartment. Usually I would arrive in time to prepare dinner, and in the mornings, after he went into his studio to paint, I would linger over coffee and feed his cat, Grande Moustache, before going back to my hotel. Yves had found her in the street, an ordinary brownish gray cat with astonishing, fierce yellow eyes that burned like blazing coals. She was wild and crazy about him. When we made love in her presence, she looked away the whole time, resigned, impassive, keeping her thoughts to herself. She was the only creature Yves allowed in his studio when he was working. All the while he was painting, she sat motionless, as if frozen in space, never changing position until he finished and signaled that she could move. When he wrote his essays and poetry, Grande Moustache would pace noiselessly along the long table, artfully, and with the precision of a tightrope walker, place one paw after the other, stepping around and over the stacks of papers and paints. She must have considered herself his muse.

By early autumn, we succumbed to convention and decided to marry. After all, we were madly in love. We had practically lived together for six months. Despite our diverse backgrounds and the language barrier, we were both painters and shared many interests. We thought alike and had the same reactions to people and things. Besides, it was 1960;

"living in sin" was against all the rules. The meddlesome concierge in Yves' apartment building glowered at me each time I arrived in the evening and demanded to know whom I had come to see—as if, after all these months, she didn't know—and disguising the arrangement from my parents was a constant challenge. I was running out of excuses to explain why I was never at the hotel when they telephoned, and they were getting suspicious. Marriage, we concluded, was the solution to all our problems.

The wedding was a simple affair at *le mairie,* the justice of the peace, followed by a reception for a few close friends and family at the Closerie des Lilas, a popular meeting place on the Left Bank for artists and writers. After recovering from the initial shock of my marrying a Frenchman, my family was eager to come to Paris for the occasion. Yves shrewdly invited a silvery-voiced baron, his wife the baronne, and a distinguished-looking marquis to the reception. After having her hand kissed with savoir faire and regularity, my mother was reassured that I was in good company. Thankful I had not been seduced into the bohemian life, she was eager to share with her friends back in Chicago her daughter's good fortune. My father had always been wary of any man in whom I showed interest. But I was a married woman now. He allowed himself to be charmed by Yves' mother and was won over by Yves; they sealed a mutual and lasting friendship. My sister was delighted to show off her college French and was in constant demand as translator, since my family spoke no French and Yves' family spoke no English. Everyone communicated through smiles and gestures, generously lubricated with champagne, and in spite of my apprehensions, the event was a success.

I was now Madame Drumont. "Drumont." I repeated my new name over and over. It had the throaty *rrrrr*, the puckered *u*, and the nasal *on*—all the impossible French sounds tucked into one word. Unfortunately, I couldn't pronounce it. Nevertheless, I was in heaven. I was born to be married to an artist. My destiny had been fulfilled. Or so it seemed.

3

The Animal Kingdom

WITH THE THAWING OF THE FRIGID WINTER of 1964 in Paris, a letter, painstakingly written, arrived from Monsieur Blevenec.

"We have begun construction on La Sallette," he wrote. "*Merci bien* for your down payment. You and your family can move into the house by the stable whenever you're ready. À *bientôt*."

"You sent a down payment? Without telling me?" Holding back tears, I asked myself, is this the man I married? Had I unwittingly fallen for a despot who wouldn't even consult me on decisions vital to us both? Had he never heard of woman's suffrage? I was beside myself. "You really want us to spend the rest of our summers in that broken-down, miserable, oversized wreck?" I cried.

"Calm down, *chérie*. Someday you'll thank me."

"Never."

"You'll get used to it."

"*Never!*"

"You have to. You have no choice."

I winced.

At this point, Yves reminded me that we had been married in France, and under Napoleonic law, the husband is considered the *lieu conjugal*. "That means," he explained with a roguish grin, "a wife is obliged to follow her spouse— me, in our case—wherever he decides to go, anywhere in the world. Whether she likes it or not." He pulled me down to his lap.

"Anywhere?" I asked incredulously.

"That's the law, *ma chérie*. Anywhere. Unless, of course, he decides to live in a dangerous place."

"What's more dangerous than living on dirt floors and getting stampeded by cows every time we go outdoors?"

Amidst kisses and caresses, I struggled to go on protesting, but it was useless. At the first sign of spring, we loaded our new car, an oversize Volkswagen camionette with elevated seats like a cross-country truck and roomy enough to transfer our household back and forth to the country. While I continued to mutter under my breath about the perversity of the Napoleonic law, Yves, Danielle, and I climbed aboard and set off for the Morbihan at dawn.

By early afternoon we had entered the heart of Brittany with its hollowed-out paths, ancient villages, forests, and farmland. Spring had come early that year. Hedges and roadsides were blooming with the golden bell-shaped flowers of the *genêt*, a spiny shrub that mingled with the more delicate yellows of forsythia. Fields of mustard colza plants flowered next to lush meadows, transforming the landscape into a green and yellow checkerboard that undulated like an embroidered quilt over the countryside. Nearing La

Salle, we turned onto an unpaved road that ran alongside a meadow. Without warning, a cart drawn by two oxen emerged from a path shrouded by overgrown hedges. A tall, broad-shouldered man held the reins in the stance of a Roman charioteer, crossed the road, and passed enigmatically onto another field.

"Wake up, honey," I said, nudging Danielle from a mid-afternoon nap. "Look over there. Those are oxen."

Except for pictures in a high school geography book, I had never seen oxen before. To see a pair of them, their powerful heads hunched and their muscular bodies straining across the field, was like reaching my hand into a distant and unknown past. Yves said that peasants in this part of the Brittany still used the farming methods of the Middle Ages. Mesmerized, I watched the cart disappear into the distance as if it were a fading mirage in the Sahara and wondered how far from the world I knew we were heading.

A deceptively romantic afternoon light bathed the houses in an apricot-tinged glow when we drove into La Salle. Nothing, however, could obscure the wreckage beneath, and my original misgivings resurfaced the minute we lowered ourselves from the lofty seats of the camionette into the courtyard. Other than Madame Blevenec's father, who was stooped over in the vegetable garden, the village was empty. Monsieur Allanic hobbled to the fence to greet us. Wiping his hands on his overalls, which emitted the pungent smell of fresh manure, he reached across the wooden posts to shake hands. His leathery face cracked into a toothless smile, and he said something unintelligible, which I assumed was in Gallo. It was hard enough for me to understand someone speaking French with all its feminine and masculine nouns, irregular verbs, and unfathomable pronunciation and grammar. I could manage when one person spoke at a time, but in a crowd, or when someone spoke the local patois, I floundered.

"We're moving into the house over there," said Yves brightly. "It should be ready by now."

Monsieur Allanic scratched the stubble on his chin. He said something about a couple of guys from Theix coming by and never getting much of anything done.

The "guys" he referred to were a mason and plumber from a nearby village whom Monsieur Blevenec had recommended for laying a tile floor and installing plumbing in the temporary house. Yves had telephoned them from Paris and had exacted a promise that the work would be finished in time for our arrival in the spring. Obviously the work hadn't begun. Scattered everywhere were pyramids of rust-colored tiles but not one was laid in place. In the middle of the room lay broken tools and old parts destined for an eventual toilet, and there was no sign of a sink. Fuming, I groped in vain for four-letter French words while Yves inspected a corner of the room designated as a kitchen.

"Look over here," he sang out. "These must be the plumber's markings for a sink. I'll make sure they finish by the end of next week." He drew me to him. "Don't worry, Mijoux. Everything's going to work out. I'll dig a hole in the woods behind the house that we can use until the plumber installs a toilet."

I watched as he grabbed a spade leaning against the wall and headed for the woods and, in spite of myself, I couldn't help admiring his long artist's fingers and his strikingly Gallic profile with an uneven nose that gave his face character.

Strong and muscular, he moved with the feline grace of a dancer, and after three years of marriage, this sensitive, unpredictable poet was still the most exciting and appealing man I had ever known. The digression, however, was short-lived. The moment he was out of sight I sank down on the doorstep. "What are we doing in this godforsaken place? I want to go back to Paris. I want to go home," I wailed with plaintive emphasis on "home."

Danielle sat beside me on the doorstep. Her long chestnut-colored hair brushed against my cheek and her gold-specked eyes gazed into mine. Pouting to mirror my expression, she nuzzled close to me, as she often did, like a cat rubbing against my leg to signal its presence. Gratefully I slid my arm around her.

"*Venez ici!*" shouted Monsieur Allanic, waving at us with both arms from the gate of the vegetable garden. Standing next to him by the fence was the woman I had seen before. She was dressed the same way I remembered her, all in black, with a long skirt and an olive green apron wrapped around her waist. A small black and white mongrel dog hopped from side to side on hind legs, yapping at her heels.

With a mixture of curiosity and trepidation, I took Danielle's hand, and we crossed the courtyard. Coming near, I overheard them speaking a harsh-sounding, guttural language. "That's Gallo," I whispered. "Maybe that's all she speaks."

"This here's Jeanne Montrelay," Monsieur Allanic called out in French as we approached. "But everyone calls her Mémé."

"*Demad. Bonjour,*" the woman said in a high-pitched voice as if straining to be heard over the wind. She squinted.

33

"I saw you once before," she said, and then she said something I didn't understand at all. Her voice lowered an octave, and she added, in French, "Old Martin here tells me you're moving into the village."

She patted Danielle on the head and reached out a sandpapery hand to shake mine. She was shorter than I remembered her. Slightly bent from a lifetime of working in the fields, she made me think of a gnome that had emerged from the pine forest hovering over the village. She appeared to be in her late sixties, although it was hard to tell. She pointed to a small farmhouse across the road and beyond a hedge. "Marcel and me. We live over there." She said something I didn't catch to Monsieur Allanic, nudged him with her elbow, and the corners of her mouth drew up into a grin, deepening the network of wrinkles that lined her cheeks.

At that instant, my heart stopped. Lumbering up the hill, with an eerie, nebulous cloud of flies buzzing overhead, were ten impassive cows, although as far as I was concerned, it could have been a herd of hundreds. Walking alongside them, waving a stick, and calling each by name was Madame Blevenec, while a little girl with straw-colored hair cropped around her ears and not much older than Danielle took up the rear, shouting orders and guiding them into the courtyard.

"Will they hurt us?" asked Danielle, slipping her hand in mine.

Jeanne Montrelay moved quickly beside us. "Looks like neither of you ever saw a cow up close before. *N'aie pas peur, petite*," she said to Danielle. "Don't be afraid. They're big, but they don't bite." She called to the little girl. "Good job, Monique. Look here. Someone new at La Salle for you to play with."

Turning to me, she said something, but she spoke so fast and clipped her words that again, I didn't understand. Then she added, more slowly, "Don't you worry about the cows, Madame Drumont. You'll be eating them long before they'll be eating you."

"But—but they kick, don't they?"

"*Dame,* no. Only if it helps 'em get out another liter of milk."

After the cows had turned into the stable and were safely enclosed for the night, Jeanne Montrelay said *"Kenavo,"* which I supposed meant goodbye in Gallo, turned and walked slowly across the road, the black and white mongrel dog trotting along at her side.

At Yves' insistence, by the end of the following week the mason completed an inexact and careless installation of a tile floor and the plumber installed an occasionally functional toilet in the corner of an adjoining building. For some inexplicable reason, he perched it at the top of several steep steps, bringing it perilously close to a low ceiling and requiring unwavering caution going up and down. Nevertheless, I was thankful not to have to grope my way into the woods after dark. Next, I explained to the plumber the kind of sink I needed: oxidized metal, eight inches deep, positioned high enough for someone of my height. The following day he arrived with a cracked, obviously second-hand three-inch-deep white enamel sink. Slinging it over his shoulder, he shuffled past me into the house. "Just don't use it for washing vegetables, clothes, or dishes," he threw back at me.

"Then what's it for?" I shouted after him. When he reappeared, he dragged his feet to the back of his pickup truck and unloaded narrow, rust-encrusted pipes. He then set about boring a hole in the meter-thick wall of our kitchen area and led the flimsy, exposed pipes through the hole, where they zigzagged along the edge of the house until they emptied into the courtyard.

"Won't these freeze in the winter?" I asked. He mumbled something inaudible.

After he left I sat at the kitchen table, glowering at the sink and washing and dicing vegetables in a bucket of water. "Merde," I swore and kicked the bucket aside. "Come on, Danielle. Let's get out of here!"

Across the road, our neighbor was in her garden. While I never admitted it, I was at first intimidated by the villagers, especially the elderly ones whom I could barely understand. Besides, Yves said city people like us would always be outsiders in the country, and I shuddered to think how the entire village must be laughing at the dainty American lady who almost fainted at the sight of a cow. "What have I got to lose?" I shrugged. "Maybe she has eggs to sell." We crossed the road.

Jeanne Montrelay leaned her shovel against a tree. "Eggs? *Dame, oui.* Come with me."

We followed her into the stable. She nodded in the direction of three cows munching hay, oblivious to our arrival.

"The brown and white one. That's Moomoot," she said as if introducing a friend. "The one next to her is La Petite Belle and the shy one in the corner is Cocotte." Noticing I was keeping a safe distance, she added, "Don't be scared, Madame Drumont. They're gentle as a baby's handshake."

Chickens that weren't scurrying around our feet were

perched on a ledge across from the cows. Our neighbor plucked the eggs from the nests, dropped them in her apron, which she had folded over and knotted into a kind of basket, and turned to me. "I've got a pot of fresh coffee brewing on the stove, and fruit juice for the little one. Come this way."

She led the way through a narrow corridor and into a small kitchen that combined the comforting smell of logs burning in the fireplace with an aromatic cabbage soup simmering in a kettle on a wood-burning stove. Danielle and I sat on a bench alongside an old worn wooden table while she brought out two cups from a cupboard, wiped them with her apron as Madame Blevenec had done, and poured drops of fruit syrup into a glass of water for Danielle.

"I see you've got workers coming around La Salle. How are things going?" She tilted her head and eyed me while pouring the strong, chicory-flavored coffee that I was becoming accustomed to into our cups. Her eyes were a deep, warm gray and gleamed with the sparkle of a much younger woman. The sun and wind had added years to her face, but through the wrinkles, her features were sharp and clear, and an image of what she might have looked like when she was young darted across my mind. As much as I resented being forced to live in a place I found so repellent, there was something about her that touched me and tempered visions of junkyards, run-down farmhouses, cows, and flies.

"It's horrible!" I blurted out before I could catch myself. "I mean, honestly, I don't know what to do about the plumber."

"*Ya!* That's Joël."

"You know him?"

"*Dame, oui.* I've known the miserable good-for-nothing since he was in diapers."

37

As long as I paid close attention, I could understand most of what she said. Or at least enough to follow the sense of the conversation. She went on, "Dumbest peasant around. I saw him driving that pile of junk he calls his van a couple of times into La Salle and asked myself what the devil was he up to. So now he calls himself a plumber. What's he screwed up this time?"

"Everything," I replied. "Last week he put in a toilet that almost never works. Today he installed a sink that can't be used for washing dishes. Or clothes. Or vegetables. It's useless!"

"Doesn't surprise me. Never knew the difference between his forehead and his backside." She leaned toward me and put a weathered hand on mine. "Between us, Madame Drumont, I wouldn't use him to paint my outhouse!"

We laughed and drank our coffee. "If you have enough eggs to sell, I'd like to buy them regularly, Madame Montrelay."

"As long as the hens do their God-given work, Madame Drumont, you can have all the eggs you need."

"Please, call me Midge."

"Mitch," she pronounced it, tapping her fist on the table. "And you call me Jeanne."

"I can't deal with him," I told Yves that night as we nestled into our mattress on the floor. "He's a local peasant who calls himself a plumber. He doesn't have the vaguest idea what he's doing."

"He's not as bad as you think, *chérie*. Besides, he does the plumbing for most of the farmers around here."

"Right, but there's no running water in the houses."

"Listen. You're a city girl. You're in the country now. You can't expect Chicago-style luxury in the backwoods of Brittany." He pulled up the covers.

"I don't."

"You do, and you're not going to get it. You have to adjust to a different way of life. You have to learn to work with these people."

"I want a decent sink, and I want a decent plumber. The neighbor who sold us the eggs has known him all his life. He's a dunce. She said so. Anyway, I can't work with him. I'll get a plumber from Vannes to do the work."

"Believe me, Midge. You'd be wasting your time. No plumber from Vannes or anywhere else around here will come this far out in the country. Forget it," he said and switched off the light.

⌒

Stirred by the soft, monotonous hum of wind whistling through the pine trees above La Salle, I rose early the next morning and drove to Vannes. Leafing through a phone book, I found the name of a construction company, Enterprise Frères Calaix, "*Toutes Services—Masons, Plombiers, Peintres.*" I drove to the address and entered a huge shed that looked like an authentic lumberyard. In the office, one of the Calaix brothers was seated behind a disorderly desk piled high with papers. Short and stocky, radiating energy, he gave me a feeling of confidence at first sight. When I told him where we lived, without hesitation he stood up, jangled his car keys, and said, "*Allons*, I'll follow you. Let's drive out and take a look."

Yves heard our cars drive into the courtyard and came
out to join us.

"*Fantastique!*" Monsieur Calaix exclaimed. "These
buildings are built to last at least another two centuries."

"They are solid," Yves said, his chest expanding.

"I'll send workmen who know the value of these old
farms," said Monsieur Calaix. We explained that we were
on a strict budget and had to find ways of restoration that
were economical.

"We'll look for shortcuts to save money," Monsieur
Calaix assured us. "We'll have to decide on covers for the
dirt floors and where to create walls. A real challenge. The
kind I like!" Before he left, we stopped by the temporary
house. I showed him my sink. "*Mon Dieu!*" he said. "I'll
send someone tomorrow to rip out this pile of junk and put
in a sink you can use. And replace these toy pipes with regu-
lation insulated pipes. I never saw anything like it!"

"This is a bigger job than we expected," Yves said as we
walked Monsieur Calaix to his car. "Perhaps we could save
in the long run if we hired an architect." Although this was
the first time he had mentioned an architect, I agreed it was
a daunting task to restore seven houses on our own.

Monsieur Calaix scribbled two names on a piece of paper. "If you decide to use an architect, you might want to
contact either of these. I've worked with them in the past,
and they are both reliable."

He drove off. Yves kissed me on the forehead. "We're on
our way, Mijoux," he said. The local team was dismissed
and never mentioned again. I congratulated myself that on
this day a flicker of hope for women's rights had prevailed in
the French countryside.

4

The Great Wall

"MODERN BUILDINGS DON'T TAKE NEAR the time it took to build these old stone houses," said Monsieur Blevenec, tapping the stone wall affectionately. "We're right on schedule for both the new house and stable. If it keeps up, we'll move into La Sallette by the end of September."

"Come into the house where it's cool," said Yves. They went inside and sat across from each other at the table. "The day you move down the hill, Monsieur Blevenec, we'll begin work on the main houses. I'm anxious to get started."

"We're all in a hurry, right, Madame Drumont?"

I nodded and poured coffee in their cups.

Three months had passed. To my surprise, life in the temporary house proved to be less horrific than I had feared. The profound quiet of the countryside, long walks with Yves through the pine forest that spread for miles and miles beyond the hamlet, glorious sunrises and sunsets that inspired the best watercolors I had ever done in my life helped me to endure the lack of comfort and the proximity to cows. The latter, thankfully, kept their distance and came and went to their private quarters with as little fanfare as possible. Best of all, the country air had transformed Danielle, who was no longer a pale Parisienne. Her face had become full and her cheeks rosy. When she stumbled, she picked herself up, brushed off the mud, and skipped off without a whimper. Unlike her mother, she romped around the animals without fear, helped feed the chickens, and "supervised" the milking of cows. As Yves had predicted, she and the youngest of the Blevenec children had become instant playmates.

Danielle climbed on the bench next to her father. With a solemn air she asked Monsieur Blevenec, "When is Monique moving?"

"Not right away, Danielle," he reassured her. "But even then, she won't be far away. Just down the hill."

A month before the last prefabricated walls of La Sallette were to be pounded into place, Monsieur Blevenec passed the word around that after Mass on Sunday, he would tear down the gigantic storehouse that dominated the courtyard of La Salle. Having lived in its shadow all summer long, I knew it intimately. It had sprung from remnants of an old stone wall. Cement had been plastered over the stones, and huge wooden beams were stationed at intervals to bolster aluminum slabs, which by now, rusted and rotting, functioned as a decrepit roof, a blight by any standard. Unrestrained for decades, it had proliferated, spawned additions, and mushroomed in size until it had earned the dubious reputation of being the defining landmark of the village.

Monsieur Blevenec declared that anyone who helped

with the dismantling of the shed and the transfer of tools and equipment down the hill to their new house could cart off all the stones, wood, and corrugated metal they could manage. By word of mouth, the news reached hamlets near and far and was passed on to small, isolated farms off country roads, unseen and hidden behind dense hedges. It amazed me that with no newspaper, telephone, or radio—many farms had no electricity—the news had spread so quickly. At dawn that Sunday morning, men with wheelbarrows and tractors began arriving to start work on the heroic task. All the villagers from La Salle came to help. Jeanne and Marcel came. Along a dirt path thirty meters past their farm lived Jeanne's older son, Roger; his wife, Thérèse; and their two daughters, Claudine and Jacqueline. They came to help. Jeanne's younger son, also named Marcel, and his wife, also named Thérèse, lived on a farm in a nearby village and they came to help.

Throughout the day, a steady stream of peasants drifted into the courtyard; some came on foot, some on bicycle, some by tractor. Entire families came. Some had packed a midday meal for a Sunday picnic. Others came out of curiosity, intending only to watch, and ended up pitching in. It seemed that the whole region had emptied itself into our courtyard. By midday, our half of the hamlet was crowded with local peasants, and except for infants in baskets and elderly bystanders leaning on makeshift canes, everyone was busily engaged in tearing down the shed. Like crowds of Lilliputians scrambling over a sleeping Gulliver, the men hoisted themselves over the top to disengage the roof and shimmied up the sides with hammers and screwdrivers to wrench and yank at the lower extremities. I tried to make myself useful, and Yves was everywhere, wherever an extra hand was needed. Work went on throughout the morning and afternoon hours. Excitement crescendoed as the multifaceted roof became unhinged, and finally, accompanied by the elated cries of young and old pulling it apart, one after the other, the walls came tumbling down. As the antiquated structure unraveled, an unobstructed view of rolling hills and fields unveiled itself, stretching all the way to the Atlantic Ocean on the left and to the Gulf of Morbihan on the right. When the old depository finally sank to the ground from where it had sprung and its remains lay strewn about like a fallen giant, a ribbon of sea glistened at the horizon, reflecting the approaching sunset. I was spellbound. An overwhelming amount of work remained to be done. The houses still needed monumental repairs, but all at once, I saw La Salle as if for the first time, and it took my breath away. With one sweeping gesture, the hamlet revealed itself to be a cluster of old yet sturdy farmhouses with an endless vista, proudly dominating the hillside and overseeing the countryside the way it must have been when it was first built three centuries ago.

At the same time, a peasant seemingly from nowhere arrived in the courtyard. Dressed in the traditional Breton costume of black pants and a multicolored embroidered jacket, he began playing the *biniou*, filling the air with the festive, Celtic, and to my ears, mournful sound of the bagpipe. Like a Bruegel painting come to life, men in work clothes and women in long skirts and lace coifs leaned their tools against the barn and fences and began to dance, while Monsieur and Madame Blevenec and their four children passed cider around from large makeshift containers.

Jeanne had been working throughout the day along with

everyone else, and now she threw aside her hammer and began to dance with the rest of the peasants. She tilted her head from side to side and her feet were light and quick as she danced the traditional dances of the Morbihan. It was easy to imagine her as a pretty young woman, graceful and flirtatious, dancing with a suitor. Marcel, her husband, stood back with the crowd until two of the men grabbed his arms and pushed him to the center. "What are you waiting for, old man?" one of them cried out. "Dance with your bride!" Only slightly taller than Jeanne, Marcel was stocky and robust. His face was squarish with the rough, weather-beaten look of a man who had spent his whole life outdoors. He grinned, narrowed his eyes, and took his place at Jeanne's side. While he knew the steps, his movements were stiff and it was obvious that Jeanne was the dancer in the family. I couldn't stop staring at them until Yves put his arm around my waist and led me to join in dances that neither of us knew, but no one cared. Along with the other children, Danielle skipped and twirled like a toy that had been tightly wound, never tiring as the celebration went on and on until it was nearly dark. Then, one by one, laden with all the materials and junk they had acquired, the last families straggled off to their villages and farms, and the hamlet was once again left by itself and silent. As Yves and I watched the sun setting behind the pine woods, the ocean and the gulf gleamed like beacons in the distance. It seemed that La Salle had been reborn that day.

I hadn't realized the enormity of moving an entire farm where a family had lived and worked for generations. While the Blevenecs didn't possess much in the way of personal belongings, the amount of accumulated tools and farm equipment was staggering. Moving the animals alone would have discouraged most people from changing addresses; and although the cows had been irreproachable, I had no regrets when they were led, impervious to the hubbub around them, down the hill to their shiny new quarters. It was early October, and the Blevenecs busied themselves with the final stages of the move. As when Noah loaded the ark, the cows were followed by pigs, chickens, a few turkeys, and goats. At last, the Blevenec family began their downhill safari with clothes, dishes, blankets, and cots.

Suddenly, it was over. Yves, Danielle, and I were alone. We looked around. La Salle was ours. Seven immense stone houses and seven and a half acres had never looked so big. It was exhilarating, overwhelming, terrifying. Danielle, at three and a half, was the least intimidated. With the supple, sinewy body of a miniature ballerina, she pirouetted through our newly acquired buildings to determine which of the houses best lent itself for play. I stood paralyzed while Yves ran off and returned, dragging two chairs and setting them down in front of the Blevenec house. He disappeared again to go to the house bordering the woods where Monsieur Blevenec had kept his cider mill and reappeared with a bottle of cool blanc de blanc. He uncorked it, poured it into two kitchen glasses, took me in his arms, kissed me, and toasted, "*Salut.* Here's to our new house. Well, seven to be exact. We did it, Mijoux. Now all we have to do is fix it up."

"A mere nothing," I said, clinking my glass against his.

5

True Love

YVES WASTED NO TIME. He christened his studio in the woods behind the Blevenecs' main house and immediately began working on paintings for an exhibition scheduled for the following March in Paris. Over the remains of a small shed, he built walls and a partial roof so that while his canvases would be protected from the elements, he could work in the open. He painted towering, Goyaesque creatures on the outside walls "to clear the air of any lingering evil spirits." For my studio, I chose the cider house, which was off by itself at the edge of the woods. Its slanted ceiling rose to a point high above like the vaults of a miniature cathedral, light poured in through a window overlooking the woods, and a kind of underwater silence reigned within. There in my own private world, I could concentrate as never before. Along the walls I taped watercolors I had painted of coves and inlets along the gulf. I set up oil paints, stretched a canvas, and made sketches of what I had in mind to paint. Sometimes I sat for hours, almost as if in prayer, attentive to the silence, savoring the possibilities. It was the first separate studio I had ever had in my life.

One evening there was a breathtakingly dramatic sunset. As the sun went down, Danielle played nearby while Yves and I sat side by side on the grass, both of us painting a flaming vermilion and celadon sky suspended over a shimmering meadow reaching all the way to the sea. I had always dreamed of sharing a moment like this with someone I loved. And now, it was happening. When we finished, we compared our paintings; how different our impressions were of the same scene. Mine was a watercolor that set out to capture a setting sun with a gamut of delicate to brilliant colors, each one laid over another like overlapping plates of glass. Yves had painted with gouache, using hard, jagged edges and clashing colors to achieve a beautiful, dark, and stormy elegy to the last moments of light. That evening, La Salle was magical.

Yves and I settled into a routine, and gradually, Jeanne Montrelay became a part of that routine. Whether helping to collect eggs in her stable, lingering over a cup of coffee in her kitchen, or chatting over her vegetable garden fence, I found that she had become intertwined in my daily life at La Salle. I no longer stumbled over half of what she said, although from time to time she would slip into patois and lose me completely. She would notice the quizzical look on my face, wink, and say, "Thought you spoke Gallo by now." At times I had the feeling I had broken through an invisible barrier and on the other side was this endearing woman whom I could at last understand and get to know. Occasionally in the late afternoons she would appear at our door, carrying a pot of soup or a bottle of homemade cider, and when I cooked something especially delicious for supper, I put aside a sample to take her the following day. Yves said I was wasting my time; he insisted we would always be outsiders to the villagers, and friendship with them was impossible. It was true that Jeanne and I had nothing in common. She was old enough to be my grandmother. She couldn't read or write. Except to walk three kilometers to attend Mass at the little church in Sulniac, she had never ventured outside the hamlet. I marveled that she could be content to spend her whole life in one place—especially a place as far removed from civilization as La Salle.

In fact, I never knew places as remote as our hamlet existed; I had always assumed that crowds of people and traffic jams were normal ways of life. Except for an occasional traveling vendor and the day when the storehouse was dismantled, La Salle rarely had visitors. While the isolation was hard for me to get accustomed to, it suited Yves perfectly. One of the reasons he chose a place far off in the country was to avoid being disturbed and distracted by friends and collectors dropping by as happened so frequently in Paris. At La Salle, he had his wish.

Until late one afternoon, a rotund white-haired, middle-aged schoolteacher from the town of Questembert and his diminutive wife drove into the courtyard. Having heard that two painters from Paris were spending summers in the Morbihan, they wanted to meet us and see our work.

"It isn't often that we have the luxury of two painters in our midst," said Monsieur Le Roux, introducing himself and his wife.

"Well, not exactly two painters," said Yves, smiling and leading the way to his studio. "My wife paints as a hobby. She's American."

I could hardly believe what I'd heard. But before I could react, Madame Le Roux embraced me and said, "Oh, Madame. You are American! I must tell you how grateful we were to see your boys arrive in '45. I remember it as if it were yesterday: even as we cowered in the shelter before the landing, we were thankful for the bombs you were dropping near our village."

"*C'est vrai,*" said Monsieur Le Roux. "You were our saviors, Madame Drumont. The courage it took for those boys to land on the beaches and climb those cliffs to liberate us is something we shall never forget. So many lost their lives. So many." His voice trailed off, and he shook his head.

Yves placed one canvas after the other on an easel, and we drew up chairs to admire the work he had been preparing for the upcoming show in Paris. He showed us paintings of rough landscapes with arid fields and stunted shrubs he did so well and others with groups of peasants huddled under skeletal trees and stormy skies. As much as I loved seeing his work, the words "my wife paints as a hobby" throbbed in my head, and I couldn't shake them out of my mind.

While Yves and Monsieur Le Roux were discussing painting and politics, Madame Le Roux leaned toward me and whispered, "I'd like to see what you do as well, Madame Drumont."

I led the way to the cider house, where I showed her my sketches and paintings of sunsets and the gulf.

"Madame, these are marvelous. *Merveilleux!*" She ran

to call her husband. "Henri! Come and look at madame's paintings!" Monsieur Le Roux joined us in the cider house and was as enthusiastic as his wife. After a moment, I glanced up to see Yves silhouetted in the doorway, observing us, expressionless, saying nothing.

"Why did you tell them that?" I said to him after they left. "You know painting isn't a hobby for me."

He shrugged. "It didn't mean a thing, *chérie*. It's just that I can't have people distracted when I'm showing my work."

"Okay, but we can both show our work. Our styles are completely different."

"You have to admit it was absurd the way they gushed over your watercolors."

"I was thrilled they liked them. Look. Your work is profound and important. I'm so proud of what you do, and I want you to be proud of what I do, too."

"I am, Mijoux," he said. He put his arms around me, kissed me on the mouth, and changed the subject. Why didn't I object more vehemently? Why didn't I make it unambiguously clear once and for all that I would not be set aside as a painter? At some subterranean level of consciousness, an uneasy feeling enveloped me, a vague shadow of doubt that refused to fade away. But, dazzled by true love, I swept my misgivings aside. After all, we were both artists. We were meant for each other. Being married to a painter—a *French* painter—was too good to be true.

6

The Butcher, the Baker . . .

HOURS BEFORE THE FIRST RAYS OF SUNLIGHT filtered through the morning mist, villagers at La Salle were awake and at work, milking cows, and heading to the fields. I had always loved to paint with morning light and quickly fell into the habit of rising as early as they did. Each morning when I went into the courtyard, still groggy with sleep, I could see Jeanne across the road, bent over in her vegetable garden, loosening the soil, and pulling out weeds. She would look up and wave. It was a signal for me that the day had begun.

Each day at La Salle began the same as the one before. The profound hush that enveloped the countryside was broken only occasionally by a faint rustling of the wind or the plaintive mooing of a cow whose calf had been dragged off to market. It was a sound unlike anything I had heard before. The cries pierced the silence, echoing and reverberating like ripples on still waters until little by little, as if abandoning all hope of being heard, they vanished, giving way once again to silence. At La Salle, hours rolled by unhurriedly.

The villagers never rushed. They took their time, ambled, and gestured as if they were following the beat of a distant, slow-motion drummer. Yves and I, too, were gradually weaned from our habitual, frenetic pace and lulled into the lazy rhythm of the country. Sometimes it seemed as if time stood still at La Salle, as if each moment remained frozen in time until something unexpected jarred the clock into ticking again.

Traffic sounds were so uncommon that the villagers identified the rare car that drove along the country road by the sound of its motor long before it turned up the hill and came into view. For groceries, everyone depended on mobile vendors who drove around the countryside, stopping in each hamlet or isolated farm to sell their wares. Jean Bonbon, as he was called, drove his faded blue van around the region on Tuesday and Friday afternoons. On arrival, he handed out sugary fruit-flavored candies, earning him his name and endearing him to the children. The rear of his van was lined with dilapidated oatmeal-colored shelves and boxes that bulged and spilled over with cookies, candies, cheeses, soaps, salad oil, cheap red table wine, sugar, flour, and other staples. On the days he came to La Salle, everyone in the village heard his van coughing and chugging in the distance and was waiting for him in front of Jeanne's and Marcel's farm long before he pulled into their courtyard. They crowded around the van to make their purchases and listen to whatever news or gossip he might have gleaned from other villages along his route. Marie of Locqueltas was finally getting over her bout with the flu. Folks are saying Henri Le Braz is going to sell off his farm because none of his kids wants to stay on and help. By the time the midwife got there, Benoit

Giroux's wife already had her fifth baby—*quelle misère*—another girl. Jean Bonbon's arrival was always an event, as was anything that broke the constant, day-after-day sameness of life on the farm.

Meurice, the postman, dropped by from time to time. Before we arrived, there was rarely any mail for La Salle or nearby hamlets. Mail was more frequent now, but even if Meurice had no letters to deliver, he stopped by to say hello whenever he happened to be in the vicinity. Short and mild-mannered, he had an unruly moustache that camouflaged an unmistakable lisp. Pronouncing *r*'s was especially tricky for him. Whenever he mispronounced a word, two stubby fingers sprang up to tug at the hairs of his moustache and serve as a diversionary tactic. He rode a rickety bicycle and stopped at every farmhouse where he was offered a glass or two of cider. Peering in the front door at La Salle, he would call out, *"Bonjou*, Madame Dumont." Yves explained that whenever Meurice came to the door, I had to stop whatever I was doing and offer him a glass of cider.

"But he's been drinking all day," I objected.

"You have to offer, or he'll be offended."

He never turned one down. As the day wore on, his lisp became more pronounced and his bike riding increasingly unsteady. Trying to avoid Meurice veering on the road was a challenge and should have produced countless accidents, although I never heard of one.

Far more hazardous on the road was Lucien, the aging butcher from Elven who had been driving his meats and innards from village to village for more than three decades in a beat-up and multiscarred Renault camionette. Unquestionably alcoholic, he began drinking early in the day and by noon was reckless and aggressive behind the wheel. He had two or three accidents the first summer we were at La Salle, including one that nearly demolished his car. Miraculously, he and everyone else had walked or staggered away unhurt. Squinting, doubled over the wheel of his camion-ette, his puffy, reddish face barely visible over the wheel, he charged around narrow curves at full speed, barreling down deserted country roads like a fearless racer at Le Mans. Far greater than my fear of colliding with Meurice and his bi-cycle was my dread of confronting the butcher head-on, go-ing around one of the sudden and frequent blind curves. I always hugged the right side of the road, blaring my horn as if I were maneuvering the sharp curves of the Amalfi Drive and praying that a compassionate God watched over the back roads of the Morbihan.

Two portly gendarmes from Elven were assigned to pro-tect and patrol villages from Elven to Theix and as far away as Questembert. I called them Tweedledee and Tweedledum; they did everything in unison and looked like twins, except the taller one had a potbelly and was bald. Once or twice a month they showed up to make an appearance and exchange gossip. Always refusing a glass of cider, they ceremoniously checked their watches and explained they were on duty. But there was never a crime to solve. No criminals to pursue. Nothing ever happened to test their investigatory skills, ex-cept once when an elderly peasant woman was murdered in her bed in a nearby village. This shocking and gruesome deed was committed by a wicked nephew who everyone said had gone bad after moving to the city. Home for vaca-tion, he plotted to rob his aunt as she slept, but in the middle of the night she had to pee, sat up in bed, and caught him in the act. In a fit of terror, he grabbed a kitchen knife and stabbed her to death. Then, overcome by remorse, he hugged and kissed her and tried in vain to resuscitate her. Beside himself with grief and drenched in his aunt's blood, he dragged himself to police headquarters and turned himself in to the two gendarmes, who were playing cards to pass the time. Cheated of an investigation, all that remained for them to do was arrest him, put him in a cell that had never been used, and wait for the chief of police from the county seat of Rennes to arrive and take him away. People from all around were horrified when they heard about the crime and relived it over and over. *"Sacrée misère!"* they commiserated. "The sins of the city have finally caught up with us poor folk in the country."

It was a late, brisk autumn afternoon when Monsieur Blevenec ambled up the hill from La Sallette and knocked on our door. "All the villagers are going to Roger's house tonight. Mostly we get together to *veillée* in winter, but a chill's in the air, so we figured we'd start early. You're part of the village now. You're welcome to join us."

After Monsieur Blevenec left, Yves explained that the *veillée* was an ancient custom that had its roots long before electricity existed, when winter nights were cold and dreary. Villagers huddled together at one of the farmhouses, drinking cider, telling and retelling legends and ghost stories, weaving the threads that bound them together. After an early supper, we walked passed Jeanne's and Marcel's darkened farmhouse and continued along the dirt path to Roger's house. His wife, Thérèse, greeted us at the kitchen door. I had yet to see her smile. Her brow was permanently etched in a frown, and her pinched lips changed position minimally as she spoke. Her manner made me suspect that Yves might be right about our never being accepted by the villagers. Roger waved to us from the head of a long wooden table. Their two daughters, Claudine and Jacqueline, rushed around the kitchen, filling everyone's glass with cider. Claudine, the eldest, was eight. A cascade of velvety black hair fell around her shoulders. Tall for her age and freckled, she glowed with health and energy, while Jacqueline, two years younger, had the angular features of her mother and was pale and listless. Monsieur and Madame Blevenec sat on a bench on one side of the table. Next to them were their eldest and only son, Jean, and four daughters, Huguette, Jeannine, Yolande, and Monique, in descending age. Everyone joined in the overlapping chatter, and I struggled in vain to follow the conversation. Jeanne went to the stove and peered in the oven to poke the *quatre quarts*, a simple cake that every peasant woman in Brittany made, to see if it was done. Claudine ran to her.

"Tell us a story, Mémé."

"Not now, *ma fille*," Jeanne said, her cheeks flushed from the heat of the oven. "Your mother needs my help."

"I can manage well enough by myself," Thérèse said sharply. Turning to everyone, she shrugged and added, "Like always, Mémé wants to be coaxed."

"Come on, Mémé," someone shouted.

"*Vas-y!*" someone else cried out.

"Just make sure it's not one of your far-fetched concoctions like the last time," called out Monsieur Blevenec, wagging a finger.

"Joseph's right, Mémé," said Roger. "You had us rolled in flour and fried!"

"To a crisp," added Monsieur Blevenec, chuckling.

"That's when you're the tastiest, Joseph Blevenec," Jeanne said and slapped the side of her thigh.

She returned to the table and settled at her place on the bench. Savoring the limelight, she took a sip of coffee and wiped her mouth with the back of her hand. "Years ago," she began, "old man Fotreau and his wife, Annick, lived on a farm in the village down the road from ours. They were getting on in years, but hard as they tried, they never had kids of their own."

"Maybe no one showed 'em how," exclaimed Roger, standing and unbuckling his belt as if he were about to drop his pants. Everyone cheered.

Jeanne held up both hands to quiet everyone down. "The closest of kin was a nephew, a mean sonofabitch with wild bushy hair that looked more like a haystack than a head o' hair. Well, one day old man Fotreau wakes up and dies. Never been a secret how miserable a woman is alone on a farm, and Annick's crying like a cloudburst when the tricky nephew appears at the door. He says with a honey-coated tongue that he'll stay and help out with the chores. Annick can't stand the sight of him, but she's feeble from grieving and caves in.

"Now, helping out isn't what the greedy bastard has in mind. All he does is milk the cows and gather eggs while she's scrubbing up after him, cooking for him, and you can bet your bottom who's doing all the work in the vegetable garden, the stable, and the fields. If she thought she knew misery before, *dame*, she's in bed with him now. By now, old man

Fotreau sees the trouble she's got herself into and sets about figuring out how to set things right for his poor Annick."

"Thought he was dead," said Thérèse dryly.

"Dead as can be," said Jeanne emphatically and rubbed her fingers and thumbs together as if she were squeezing a cow's teats. "That night, old man Fotreau puts a hex on the cows so the next morning they squirt out milk that's sour-smelling and spoiled. 'If he can't sell the milk, he'll think the farm's worthless and move on,' he chuckles to himself. 'Once he's gone, *dame*, the milk will be sweet-smelling like before.'"

"Mémé's off again," said Roger.

"Shhh," said Claudine.

Jeanne leaned forward. "Instead of moving on, the sonofabitch tells Annick that from now on, she'll be milking the cows along with all the other work she's been doing. When old man Fotreau sees this, he puts a spell on the chickens so the next morning, they lay eggs—rotten by the dozen. 'You moldy old scoundrel,' shouts the nephew, shaking his fist to the heavens. 'I'm on to your tricks. No matter what, I'll never leave this place. I'm staying—forever!' Straightaway he puts the old lady to work collecting eggs. Now she's doing everything while the nephew sits on his rump in Fotreau's old chair by the fireplace getting fatter and lazier by the minute."

Jeanne leaned back and her eyes rolled upward. "That night, *mes enfants*, I'll never forget it. Dogs were howling. Lightning and thunder were so frightful they woke up every living creature. Except for the nephew, who had eaten and drunk himself into a stupor. When he wakes up, he wails, 'Aiyee! Wha' 'appen?' He can't talk right 'cause in the middle of the night, every last one of his teeth fell out of his gums and scattered over the bedsheets. And if that wasn't trouble enough, the next day at supper, his left eye pops out of its socket and lands smack in the cabbage soup."

"Ooooh, gross!" squealed Jacqueline and covered her eyes.

"That's scary," said Danielle.

"Nothing to be scared of, *petite*," said Jeanne. "*Mes enfants*, I saw it with my own eyes. He was toothless as a newborn and wore a patch over his left eye. One day it's an arm that pops off. Next day, a leg. I won't go on about all his parts falling off, but old lady Fotreau is spending her time sweeping 'em up with a broom. By the end of the summer, there's nothing left of him except his clothes, his hat, and his bushy hair. You know what Annick did?"

Jeanne paused, looked around, and clasped her hands. "Well, *dame*, she stuffed him and hung him on a pole in the garden, where you can see him to this day, yelping and flapping in the wind, scaring the devil out of the crows!"

Everyone clapped or groaned. Claudine jumped up and hugged her. Jeanne looked over at me and winked. How I loved watching her. She was unpredictable and irreverent. Her eyes gleamed, and her face made me think of the sun, glowing, radiating warmth, illuminating everything around her.

Thérèse and Claudine served cake and poured coffee, while everyone laughed, joked, and retold outrageous parts of stories Jeanne had told in the past. After a while, the conversation turned to the weather and became serious.

"How long can we wait, Roger?" said Monsieur Blevenec. "God knows, the ground is dry as bones under an August sun."

Marcel shook his head. "If we don't get rain pretty soon, it will be the worse for our cabbages."

"We peasants would die out in a minute without our cabbages," said Jeanne. She referred to herself as a peasant, as did everyone else in the village, except for Monsieur Blevenec, who called himself an agricultural worker. At first, I thought it was pretentious of him. Later, I realized he was a dreamer and yearned to better his station in life. Yves said the word "peasant" concealed a hint of self-deprecation. I never discerned it, perhaps because, as he said, the last thing one understands in a foreign language is nuance.

"There's no relief in sight," said Roger.

"We'll get to know misery this year," said Marcel. Everyone nodded in agreement. I had heard the phrase before: *"On va connaître la misère!"* Like the plaintive chorus of a song, it inched its way into every conversation, a constant and inescapable menace hanging overhead. In the country, life revolved around the weather, and it was rarely accommodating. So strong was the magnetic pull of the moon in the Morbihan that it seemed to hold you in its grasp like a tide being towed out to sea against its will. The villagers predicted the weather from moon cycles or by gazing at the shape of the moon or the glow around it. Sharp edges promised sunshine; haze around the moon signaled rain. They lamented a dry spell that devastated the fields, whereas too much rain flooded the fields, spoiled the crops and ruined the harvest. Life swung precariously between two extremes. Forever dependent on forces beyond their control, the peasants resigned themselves to fate. If they couldn't harness the weather, how could they control the other vagaries of life?

It was late. Roger pushed his chair from the table, stood

up, and stretched. "Tomorrow morning starts at sunrise for my cows, *mes amis*, just like every other day."

"My cows don't sleep late either, son. *Nozvad*," said Jeanne in Gallo, slapped the table, and got up to leave.

Everyone said good night. The villagers kissed each other twice on each cheek—four kisses in all. Yves, Danielle, and I shook hands with everyone and found our way home in the dark.

7

Ghosts from the Past

OUR FAVORITE RESTAURANT IN VANNES served the most sumptuous *plateau de fruits de mer* I had ever tasted, and it was
there I had the life-altering encounter with delicately poached
langoustines dipped in freshly made mayonnaise. The dining room was decorated in an uncluttered, rustic style that
appealed to both Yves and me. Upon inquiry, we were told
that an architect from Vannes, Maître Guerain, had designed and restructured the restaurant. Assuming it was an
oversight by Monsieur Calaix not to have mentioned him,
Yves called the architect the next day and invited him to La
Salle to look over the property. Suave, with prematurely
white hair and chiseled features, he exuded confidence. Gesturing with graceful, manicured hands, he looked like a
high priest bestowing benediction. "This is precisely the sort
of project I do best," he assured us. It was decided; we now
had an architect to supervise the restoration and Enterprise
Frères Calaix to do the work.

There was silence, however, at the other end of the phone

when I told Monsieur Calaix we had hired Maître Guerain as our architect. Finally he said, "I regret, madame, but I suspect Maître Guerain will prefer to chose his own team of workers."

"It's a question of jealousy," explained Yves. "It happens all the time in small towns. We have no choice. We have to go along with the architect's wishes."

But troubling information began to surface regarding Maître Guerain's past. We heard by chance that after the war, he had served time in prison.

"Just what we need," I moaned. "A felon to supervise the work."

"It was probably political," Yves said. "Listen, the German occupation tore this country apart. Most people were brave and resisted the Germans; but others figured that the occupying armies were the victors, and they wanted to be on the winning side." He went on to say that a small percentage of Frenchmen even joined the infamous French battalions that fought alongside the Germans and were dispatched to the Eastern Front. The Germans treated them as cannon fodder and sent them to the battle of Stalingrad. Most of them perished. Those who survived made their way back to France, sometimes on foot, where they were looked upon as traitors, faced the wrath of their countrymen, and went into hiding or changed identities. After the war, many who were guilty of collaborating with the occupying German armies were captured and punished. Women who had slept with German soldiers had their hair shaved off and were publicly humiliated. Some were accused falsely, based on jealousies or personal vendettas. Many were imprisoned, often unjustly. Families were split, lifelong friendships destroyed.

"When the war was over," Yves said, clenching his fist, "everyone claimed to have been a hero in the Resistance. But many lied about what they did or didn't do during the war. If you believed everything you heard, you would think that no one had sympathized with the Germans, that no one had collaborated. And many of those who were accused of collaborating were innocent!" He went on and on. He had grown up during that period, and I had never seen him so emotional. I listened, fascinated. I'd had no idea how wrenching the war and occupation had been for the people who lived through it.

In the end, Yves and I concluded that Guerain had probably been a victim of professional jealousy, and we determined to disregard the rumors circling around our maverick architect's past. The following week we met in his office. He had drawn up final plans that appeared plausible and reasonable. We signed the contract. Heading back to La Salle, Yves drove the camionette, and I joined Maître Guerain in his swift, luxurious black Mercedes. Along peaceful country roads, the conversation shifted to politics.

"Of course, madame, as an American, you may not be aware how regrettable it was that after the war, Brittany remained under French domination." Puzzled by his choice of words, I remembered what Yves had told me about how divisive the occupation had been, especially in Brittany, where a small but passionate independence movement had existed for years. Breton Libre, as it was known, had led the Germans to believe they would be welcomed as saviors by the people in Brittany. For the most part, they were mistaken.

"Those were painful years, *chère madame,*" Guerain rambled on. "But the Germans brought us great hope when they arrived to liberate us."

"To *liberate* you?"

"*Mais oui.* Unfortunately they did not succeed, but rest assured the job will one day be finished."

Wait a minute, I thought to myself. Is he saying what I think he's saying?

He went on, blithely reminiscing about the occupation and to my soaring consternation, about the inspiring example of German soldiers to the young people of Brittany. Then, after a brief moment of reflection, his face assumed a beatific glow. "Some day the world will come to appreciate the exceptional moral leadership it was granted under the reign of Adolf Hitler."

I gasped. He was a Nazi collaborator!

We arrived ahead of Yves; the camionette was no match for the Mercedes. The minute Yves drove into the courtyard, I pulled him aside while Maître Guerain strutted imperiously around the property.

"What's wrong, *chérie*?" said Yves. "You're pale."

"Look at him parading about. In knee-high boots! Like a concentration camp commander! How could we have been so blind?"

"Mijoux. What's wrong? What happened?"

I repeated the conversation. "I . . . I can't believe he's fixing up our house," I stammered. "I've never been religious, but I swear I hear a chorus of Jewish ancestors wailing on the hill!"

"He's not worth your tears, *chérie*. Of course we don't want him to work on La Salle. We don't want him ever to set foot on our property."

"But we signed the damned contract!"

"We'll pay for the plans and tell him our funds dried up. Besides, maybe we don't need an architect. If we can manage with Frères Calaix, think of the money we'll save!"

It was settled. Maître Guerain was dismissed, Frères Calaix rehired, and the ancestral wailing mingled with the wind whistling through the pine trees and faded away. The excruciating wounds France suffered during the war years had been reopened before my eyes. In spite of passage of time, the poison beneath the surface had continued to fester and would not disappear.

Until the arrival of workmen from the Calaix brothers' shop, the idea of restoring half of a hamlet had been an abstraction, a project safely consigned to blueprints, a challenge to be confronted at some vague future date. Now, suddenly, the amount of work needed to restore La Salle was a reality and loomed over us like a ghostly shadow of the old depository. Yves became more anxious than I had ever seen him before. He worried about everything: Could we manage without an architect? Would our funds cover the rising costs? How could he possibly finish the required number of paintings in time for his show in Paris?

One evening, after a long and frustrating day in his studio, he stormed into the kitchen as I was preparing supper. "We have to talk," he said.

"What is it, *chéri*?"

"I won't be involved in the restoration of La Salle any longer. You'll have to supervise the work on your own."

"But, Yves, I couldn't possibly do it on my own."

"Look, I'm preparing for a show. Once the show is over, things will be different. But for now, I have to concentrate on my painting."

"Of course you do. But as long as we share the work on the house, it won't be so much of a burden."

"I don't want to hear about it. From now on, it's your house. You fix it up."

"What?"

"I've made up my mind."

"But, Yves—"

"That's final."

Somehow, before Danielle awoke in the mornings or after taking her to school, after doing the marketing, the cleaning, and cooking, after meetings with Monsieur Calaix, and between surveying the work of the masons and carpenters, I managed to snatch brief moments to paint. Delicate morning light, nuanced and breathtaking sunsets, and the mysterious woodlands surrounding La Salle intrigued me more and more and found their way into my painting. By now the cider house had sketches taped along the walls and canvases leaning against the wall, some sketched in, a few finished. It had become my hideaway, my house of dreams.

But strains were building up between Yves and me. It seemed he resented the fact that I found time to paint, and often, when I returned from a quick cup of coffee or a glass of cider at Jeanne's house, I found him waiting impatiently for me by the road with endless questions and reproaches. Then, just as I thought my idyllic marriage was unraveling before my eyes, he burst into the cider house one afternoon with a huge vase overflowing with wildflowers. It was the most extravagant bouquet I had ever seen in my life. He wanted to see what I had been working on. He praised my watercolors. He asked me to show him my watercolor technique. His manner was as if nothing were wrong; he was charming and affectionate. Perhaps it was his showing interest in my work. Perhaps it was the gesture of offering me wildflowers or the intoxicating fragrance of the bouquet. Perhaps it was because I wanted so desperately to believe that everything was all right. Whatever it was, my fears evaporated like dewdrops into a morning haze.

⁓

We had stayed in the country a month longer than planned. The weather turned cold. Work on La Salle slowed down. Yves chopped wood for our fireplace, and thickening mists and chills of late October signaled a return to city life.

8

A Few Red Dots

OUR APARTMENT WAS BETWEEN DENFERT-ROCHEREAU and the Place d'Italie and faced the Métro tracks, which emerged aboveground for a few stations before retreating into the nether labyrinth of Paris. Every four minutes a train rumbled past our windows, causing the building to shake with such unswerving regularity that even if a train missed its run, I trembled on schedule. Over the summer months, I had almost forgotten the bustle and clamor of Paris. Now the city seemed noisier than ever. That winter, Paris was enveloped in a spray of drizzle known as *la petite pluie*. Occasional glimmers of light contrived to slip through the bleak clouds, and after interminable weeks of sunshine deprivation, I felt a seething urge to paint murals on the dreary gray walls of the Métro stations. They would be wild, ecstatic splashes of cadmium and chrome yellows, reverberating from one Métro stop to the next like a tribal medicine man's invocation to the sun to rise again, an audacious artistic statement that would jostle the complacent Parisian art world and force it to take note of me. But, like so many others before it, the project never left the rumpled pages of my sketchbook; I was too busy juggling the vying roles of wife, mother, and artist. Besides, in Paris, I had no place of my own to paint. Yves' studio took up most of the space in our apartment; next to it was the kitchen, a small dining room, and two small bedrooms—ours and Danielle's. I worked mostly outdoors, although sometimes I sketched or put finishing touches on a painting in the kitchen. How I missed the cider house! But after all, I reassured myself, Paul Klee had painted in the kitchen and had turned out masterpieces, although I wondered if Madame Klee had been as annoyed as Yves sometimes was upon finding messy paints strewn over the kitchen table.

It wasn't the first time I had tried to balance art with life. In Chicago, I had worked at a myriad of jobs, rising at dawn to paint and rushing home after work to resume painting until midnight. Yves had never done anything but paint. He was the most disciplined artist I had ever known. Even during the years when he rarely sold a painting, he refused to get outside work to support himself. His rent-controlled apartment was one of many reserved by the city of Paris for painters, sculptors, and their families, allowing us to live virtually rent-free. By the time we met, he was making a modest living through his painting. Painting was all that mattered to him. How well I understood. I, too, found myself constantly thinking about a canvas I was working on or dreaming about the one I had yet to begin. Sometimes I wondered from where sprang that endless compulsion to create works of art. Did those early Cro-Magnon artists skip meals, forget to go to bed, and ignore all else to

finish a series of bulls and bison cavorting on the caves of
Lascaux?

Yves' exhibition had been arranged by Barnet Conlan, an
art critic who had followed Yves' career for years, had written articles about his work, and had given him constant encouragement. A gentle, cultured Irish poet, he wrote a weekly
column for the *London Daily Mail* about the Paris art scene
and had known every artist over the years from Picasso to
Amedeo Modigliani to Fernand Léger. While he wasn't an
influential critic in the contemporary art world, he was re-
garded with respect and affection. Nearing eighty, he was
tall and extremely thin, as he believed people should eat less
and less as they grew older. With an uncanny ability to envi-
sion what a painter would be doing long before the artist
himself was aware of the direction, he was devoted to artists
he believed in. Yves was one of a select few. The show was
scheduled for the first two weeks in March at the Galerie
Rive Droite, and Yves was under ever-increasing pressure to
finish the required number of paintings. The gallery printed
invitations; we had posters printed, reproducing Yves' magnificent painting of a pheasant standing regally against a
shimmering background of wheat or grass, painted in rich,
vibrant colors.

Two friends offered to help with preparations for the
show. One, of course, was Le Guerrec, who went back to
Yves' student days at the École des Beaux-Arts. Le Guerrec
personified everything I imagined a bohemian artist to be.
He spoke an unintelligible argot, and judging from the reac-

tion of those around him, his vocabulary must have been scandalous. So was his appearance. One day he would wear oversize baggy pants and a transparent top. A day later, he would appear in a racy halter, skintight, flaming pink pants, and a hairdo that defied gravity. As for table manners, it was best not to eat with him in public. He fractured every rule of propriety from ear-shattering belching to eating directly from his plate without the intervention of forks or knives. I had never seen anyone like him in my life. But he was a loyal friend; he was generous, funny, and since it was thanks to the vernissage of his art show that I had met Yves in the first place, I had great affection for him.

The other friend was David, a young Scottish lad who had recently entered our lives. Tall, lanky, freckled, with a bright crimson ponytail and a scraggly goatee, David stood out like a beacon in any French crowd. His family in Aberdeen had disowned him the day he left for Paris to paint; he was penniless but undaunted and had adopted Yves as his mentor. One evening he brought a stack of his drawings and paintings to our studio. One by one, he held up sensitive, dreamlike pastels of Scottish cityscapes, landscapes, and imaginary country scenes, and peering from behind each paper or canvas, he eagerly awaited our judgment. Both Yves and I praised his work and urged him to devote himself to his art. Considering his family's fierce opposition to his painting, we wondered if this might have been one of the few times he received any support or accolades for his endeavors. By coincidence or by design, he invariably arrived at our doorstep in time for meals. The speed at which he devoured whatever I served made me suspect these might be his only meals, although he assured me he was far from being a starving artist. He spent more and more time with us. Danielle adored him; it was as if he were one of the family.

Le Guerrec, David, and I spent days distributing posters in cafés, bistros, and galleries. An incongruous threesome, we raised French eyebrows as we tacked up posters in shops and restaurants on the Left Bank, the Right Bank, and in the neighborhood where the exhibition was to take place. Parisian shopkeepers and restaurant owners rarely refused a poster; the challenge was to find a blank space in windows or along walls already overcrowded with them. David was expert at crawling along windowsills with catlike dexterity to uncover the last remaining spot for a poster. I wrote Yves' bio for the invitations. Le Guerrec helped send them out, and David and I ran errands and delivered finished paintings to the framers. They were frenetic, exhilarating days. We were all excited about Yves' show.

The Galerie Rive Droite was packed the night of the vernissage. Along with a small group of collectors were gallery opening habitués, relatives, and friends. Barnet Conlan was there, and with paternal pride introduced Yves to everyone, pointing out and praising the depth and strength of each of the paintings. David was there, waving his arms, greeting everyone with his customary exuberance, gazing with undisguised worship at each of Yves' paintings, his bright red hair and goatee blazing like torches in the night sky. And Le Guerrec was there, looking like a bedraggled beatnik and unsettling everyone in earshot with his shameless argot. Checkbook in hand, several potential women buyers wearing miniskirts and dragging their fur coats behind them circled around Yves, effusing over him and his new work like chickens clucking around a morning feed in a farmyard. Four paintings boasted red dots, meaning they were sold, and several others had black dots at their sides, indicating they were reserved. After turning out the lights, the gallery dealer invited Barnet, David, Le Guerrec, Yves and me, and a few lingering friends to what turned into a boisterous and euphoric celebration in a local bistro. The show would stay open for another three weeks, time enough for additional sales. The opening was a success, but Yves knew his work was not in the mainstream. It would take a miracle to attract the attention of influential critics who cared only for abstract art. Yet, in spite of the obstacles he had faced for years, he never doubted himself. Perhaps the fact that he was not accepted in the established art world made him even more tenacious and single-minded. At least, that was the impression he gave to me.

9

Electric Power

Yves' parents were characters out of *Madame Bovary*. His father, Cyril, owned one of the largest pharmacies in Paris and bragged that he had never offered a gift to anyone in his life, nor had he ever lifted a finger to help his wife, Maude, not even when she was sick or pregnant. Maude, a tall and determined woman with strong, aquiline features, had dreamed of becoming a nun from the time she was a young girl. To her dismay, her father, a well-to-do manufacturer of French berets and a devout anticleric, insisted she marry. In the end, she agreed to marry Cyril, whom she considered an uninspiring candidate with one redeeming quality: he attended Mass every Sunday. He was won over by a hefty dowry that paid for his first pharmacy. To solidify the shaky foundations of the union, Cyril wasted no time impregnating his bride. Yves was born, and two more sons followed in rapid succession. As the boys were growing up, Maude drummed into them that her first love was the Church and that as soon as their father died, she would en-

ter a convent. By the time Cyril, whose health was impeccable, departed fifty years later, her passion to be a nun had
faded into a dim, girlish fancy. Never suited to staying home
and raising children, she hired maids and governesses to do
the job while she diverted herself with a shop of antiques
and baubles on the Place des Vosges. Yves, being the first-
born, was given special attention, and maids were instructed
never to contradict him. Master Yves learned early on to
have his own way.

I was the first non-Frenchperson admitted into the family, and fitting in wasn't easy. One of the hardest things to
adjust to was the French custom of using the formal *vous* or
the friendlier *tu* for the word "you." Yves' parents said *tu*
when talking to grandchildren, maids, cats, dogs, chickens,
and other domesticated animals, but they addressed their
daughters-in-law as *vous*. "My brothers' wives aren't offended," observed Yves. "They're French; they understand
vous is a sign of respect."

"Respect!" I grumbled. The word sounded aloof to me, a
verbal barricade shouting: "Keep your distance in *this* family!" Nevertheless, they showed affection in other ways, and
after a while, I grew accustomed to being called *vous*. Besides, I had a sense of belonging in France in a way I had
never felt before and would never fully understand. For one
thing, France seemed to me to be the ideal place for a painter.
Spirits of artists past encircled me. Their presence was so pal-
pable that I felt I could reach out and touch Van Gogh or Pissarro or Berthe Morisot as if they were strolling alongside
me, deep in conversation about a painting with which one of
us was struggling. An artist—even a self-doubting one like
me—was *somebody* here. When people passed by as I sketched

the Place de Furstenberg or the Jardin du Luxembourg, they nodded, but never disturbed my concentration. By now I had become relatively fluent in the language and had come to admire the strength of tradition that cemented French families and society together. From the start, I never thought of myself as a foreigner. Living in France, whether in Paris or in the country, seemed right for me, as if it were meant to be, much the same way it was my destiny to be an artist and to be married to Yves.

Yet, in those early years, life vacillated more and more without warning between the idyllic and the intolerable. There were times when Yves became so unreasonable that I told myself I must leave, although I had no idea where to go. Then, the next moment, life would be dizzily romantic as if marriage hadn't dimmed the ardor that ignited our time together. When he called me his sorceress, his lioness who traveled across the plain with him, his inspiration, his great love, I forgot the tension and doubts of the day before and trusted once again that he was my partner for life. When we had guests, we exchanged secret glances and devised discreet signals under the table to reassure each other that soon they would leave and we would be alone together again. At times like these, it was impossible to imagine being apart from him, even for a day. We knew what the other was thinking long before the thought was put into words. We were perfectly matched. Everyone said so.

Encouraged by the response to his show, Yves was painting better than ever. His most successful paintings had a limited palette, restricted to closely related hues. His power was in the intensity of feeling, the tactile application of paint, and richly compressed color schemes. As time went by, my eye sharpened in viewing his work. Often he would call me into his studio to show me a painting in progress and ask my opinion: Was the painting finished? Did one of the parts overpower the rest? Was the figure necessary or was the painting stronger without it? I was thrilled when he valued my suggestions and put them to use. Still, I couldn't help wishing he encouraged me more in my work. I had willingly put aside my painting to help with his exhibition, but he might have been more appreciative. For instance, he might have said, "Sorry you haven't had time to paint these past months, Mijoux. You'll have a show of your own one day, and I'll be there to help."

He never said it. His suggestion that I spend less money for watercolor paper took me by surprise, and when people admired my work, as the schoolteacher from Questembert and his wife had done, I could feel resentment smoldering, masked by an expressionless look on his face. Still, I reassured myself that in time, especially when Yves received the recognition he yearned for and deserved, we would nurture each other's art and create beautiful works side by side.

"You are a woman meant to live with a genius," Yves said over breakfast one morning. Obviously this was a genuine compliment, since he considered himself to be a bona fide genius. While I had no reason to doubt him, I suspected that history would be in a better position to assign the title rather than the genius himself. Or herself. We were both in agreement, however, that he was a great painter.

"It is no longer possible," he continued in the same matter-of-fact tone, "for you to paint as well as for me to paint."

"Pass a croissant, *s'il te plaît*," I said, changing the subject.

"Were you listening? I said it is no longer possible for you to paint."

I buttered my croissant.

"Did you hear me?"

"Darling, be serious."

"I have never been more serious."

"Yves, that's absurd. You knew I was a painter when you met me and you knew it when you married me."

I went to the stove to reheat the coffee.

"Things are different now," he said in a low, controlled voice. "There is room for only one painter in this family."

"Why are things different now?" I asked, pouring coffee in his cup. "I don't get in your way. I paint outdoors. And in the country, we each have our own studio. You have yours; I have the cider house. That's one of the reasons we bought La Salle." He didn't answer. After a moment, I tried to make light of the conversation. "Listen, from now on, I'll clean up the mess on the kitchen table. Honestly." I reached across the kitchen table and put my hand on his. He snatched his hand away.

"I'm not talking about where you paint. I'm talking about *if* you paint."

"Of course I paint . . ."

"You're not listening!" His voice became agitated. "Your role in this marriage is to help me in my work, not to waste our time and money on your painting."

"Yves. Don't talk like that."

"*Tu ne comprends pas!* You don't understand! You are a woman destined to live with a genius, and you will realize yourself through my oeuvre!"

"You know I could never stop . . ."

"You don't hear me!" he shouted, shoving back the table and jumping up. "You are the lightbulb. I am the electricity." He gestured, imitating an electric current zigzagging through the air with his fingers. "Without me, you don't exist! *Moi, je suis un génie!*" He pounded the table. "I paint. You don't. In Paris, La Salle. Anywhere. That's final!"

I stared at him in disbelief. It wasn't the first time Yves had given orders like a dictator and the next minute had reverted to the tenderhearted poet with whom I had fallen in love. And yet, from the look in his eyes and the tone of his voice, I could see he meant every word. What could I say? I wanted to say that I loved the fact that he was a painter and always thought he loved the fact that I was a painter, too. I wanted to say that I had always painted, and how could he even ask such a thing. He was telling me to stop being me!

I said nothing. Was I so taken aback that I lost my voice? Was I afraid I might lose the Yves I loved so much, the Yves with whom I painted the sunset side by side, the Yves with whom I had a child, the Yves who changed my life and had made my fantasies become realities? Did I reassure myself that the love we felt for each other would soothe his anxieties, and in time, everything would be all right? Did I tell myself this mood would pass as had all the others before it, and that tomorrow he would be himself again? But I couldn't help wondering which of the changing personalities was the real Yves.

From then on, I continued to do small watercolors, which I didn't mention to anyone and kept in a small army-green portfolio that I kept out of sight in a chest of drawers, underneath my sweaters. It ripped me apart to be secretive, but how could I stop painting entirely? Color meant everything to me. The world and my emotions were translated to me through color. Regardless of where I was, whether in the country or in Paris, each rocky beach, each clearing in a pine forest, each row of cement buildings or hidden courtyard opened onto a world I was impelled to sketch or paint, to dig deep into my own vision and express what was mine alone. I had wanted to be a painter for as long as I could remember. Marrying Yves confirmed what I had hoped for and believed all along, proving that becoming a painter wasn't just an idle dream. Now suddenly, everything that seemed right and inevitable was forbidden. How could I choose between painting and the man I loved? Love—such an anemic word! It could never encompass the overwhelming attraction, the heretofore unexplored emotions that bound me to him. I had waited all my life for him. And now he had ordered me to stop painting! The thought was unbearable. I had been torn in two, bound and gagged. Painting was breathing. I was suffocating.

Barnet Conlan came to our studio once a week for dinner. His drawn, bony, and still handsome face with short brushstrokes of white strands of hair made him at seventy-nine a striking yet fragile figure. He ate rice and politely tasted small portions of anything else I had prepared. But he never refused a glass of wine and was articulate and energetic until well past two in the morning, eager to discuss philosophy; politics; social upheavals; literature; the past, present, and future of art; whatever subject arose. One evening, over dessert and coffee, Barnet looked at me quizzically and said, "I've never seen anything you do, Midge. Why don't you show me some of your work?"

"She hasn't painted for a long time," Yves cut in with a dismissive wave of his hand.

"Well then, show me what you did in the past," Barnet insisted with a searching smile.

"Sure, *chérie,* show Barnet some of your watercolors." Yves nodded patronizingly as if he were telling a three-year-old to show the drawing she had done in preschool that day. I went to the chest of drawers, uncovered the portfolio I kept out of sight, and began showing the watercolors I had done at La Salle along with those I continued doing secretly in Paris, one after the other. All the while, Yves leaned back in his chair, his face a blank, his arms folded across his chest.

Barnet pressed forward and studied them without a word. Finally his face broke into a warm, broad smile. "Why haven't you shown these to me before, Midge? These are the finest watercolors being done in Paris today. Tomorrow morning, I'm taking you around to the galleries. I want to introduce you to dealers. Your work should be known here." Catching my look of apprehension, he added, "Don't be shy about your work. Anyway, I won't accept no for an answer." I glanced at Yves. I could see he was furious. Barnet always took him around the galleries.

"Now you've done it!" he exploded after Barnet left. "What got into you?"

I gathered the watercolors and slid them back into the portfolio. I knew Yves wouldn't show his anger as long as Barnet was there. But now, rage was flashing in his eyes. "Look, Barnet asked me to show him what I did, and you said it was all right. How did I know he was going to like them? If it upsets you, I won't go."

"What do you mean, you won't go? If you don't show up, he'll think I kept you from going. You'll keep the appointment, and from now on, you will never tell anyone you paint." He held my arms at my side. "Do you understand?" His grip tightened. "You will never again show your paintings. To *anyone!*"

Making the rounds of art galleries the next day with Barnet Conlan was like being flung from one frenzied amusement park ride to another, over and over again. When he introduced me to a gallery dealer as an important contemporary American artist, I determined to dedicate myself to painting. But seconds later, Yves' words flooded back into my head, and I knew it was absurd even to think about it. We continued along the rue des Beaux-Arts and the rue de Seine, dropping into one gallery after the next. Barnet introduced me using my maiden name. "Don't use your married name," he said afterward. "You have a life of your own as an artist. You're not in the shadow of anyone." Over a café crème at La Coupole, while reviewing the events of the morning's round of galleries, he told me he was dedicating one of his poems to my watercolors. The title of the poem was *"L'Aube"* or "Dawn." "This is the dawn of a new beginning for you as an artist," he said when we shook hands and parted. Holding back tears, I watched as he wound his way, bent over and frail, through the bustling and indifferent crowds along the boulevard Montparnasse.

10

Les Quatre Quarts

I COUNTED THE DAYS until we would return to La Salle. The Paris I loved had closed in on me, and I longed for the spacious landscapes of the country, the sun filtering through the haze over the gulf, the mist hovering over the meadows, the smell of wet pine trees, the silent afternoons and evenings. Sometimes, when it became unbearable not to paint, I transported myself to the cider house and lost myself in imagining wildly extravagant canvases with dazzling colors and unheard-of shapes until a screeching sound of a siren or the clamor of a traffic snarl jolted me back to reality. Walking along busy Paris streets, I imagined Jeanne Montrelay at my side. Dressed in a long black skirt and lace coif, she would press her hands against her ears to block out the roar of the Métro. She would nudge me with her elbow and point incredulously at the towering buildings along the boulevard that jutted together so tightly they swallowed up the sky, allowing only narrow slices of light through the cracks. Having lived all her life at La Salle, where silence ruled and sky was everywhere, she would be dumbfounded by the noisy, crowded cityscape.

I missed the village. I wondered how Roger and Thérèse had gotten along through the harsh winter months. I imagined Monsieur and Madame Blevenec and their five children in their shiny new house at the bottom of the hill and wondered if the winds were howling through the shaft between the house and stable without the shield of the pine forest above them. I missed the voices of the children. I pictured Danielle rushing outside to play in the courtyard or skipping off with Monique to feed the chickens. I even missed the cows. But especially, I missed Jeanne. I missed seeing her grin and wave at me from across the road. When I was too busy or preoccupied with my own problems she seemed far away, but then she would reappear in my thoughts as palpably as if we were having long talks in her kitchen while she stoked the fire, waiting for coffee to brew. I would have written her a letter or a postcard except, of course, she couldn't read. As for telephoning, I remembered the day when Yves had telephone wires installed at La Salle and told everyone in the village they could use our telephone whenever they needed to.

"I'll use it for sure," I remembered Roger saying. "It will be a damn sight better than running around the countryside, trying to track down a doctor for the girls or a vet for a sick cow."

Marcel picked up the receiver, stared at it, turned it around, and gingerly set it down. "*Merci bien*, Yves," he said, "but we've gotten along without this contraption all these years. Can't see why we'd need it now."

Roger's face broke into a mischievous grin. "Say, Mémé,"

he teased. "Don't you want to call an old friend in Questembert and say hello?" He grabbed the telephone and pressed it against her face.

Jeanne turned pale. She jumped back as if she'd been bitten by a snake. *"Sacré diable!"* she shot back. "Don't point that thing at me, Roger Diquero. I won't go near it! I'll do my talking face-to-face, not like a crazy person shouting through a bunch of wires that any minute will blow him to hellfire and beyond!"

No, telephoning was out of the question. But I made plans. As soon as we returned to La Salle, I would take her to Vannes. *Gwenet*, as she called it, was only twelve kilometers from La Salle, yet she had never been there. I would take her shopping with me. I would show her the center of Vannes, which was crowded with shops carved out of ancient ramparts, and walk with her along the narrow streets that wound their way through massive stone archways and descended to the waterfront. I could see her round face lighting up, her gray eyes sparkling, and the corners of her mouth rising into a smile.

Yves delayed our departure that spring to follow up on contacts made at his exhibition. For two interminable months, I served tea to every art collector and art critic in Paris willing to accept an invitation. Reluctantly I packed away my oil paints and resentfully buried my watercolors and treasured sable brushes among sweaters, underpants, and bras in a bottom drawer. I couldn't wait to get back to La Salle, where there were more places to hide clandestine materials and more opportunities to steal away to paint. The first week in June, after having exhausted every possibility for promoting Yves' paintings, we loaded the camionette and were on our way.

As we turned into the courtyard, I glanced across the road and saw Jeanne rushing toward us as fast as she could. "Expected all of you months ago," she said breathlessly, hugging Danielle and greeting me with two kisses on both cheeks. "*Dame, sûr,* I was worried. Well, no matter. You're here. You're safe. All of you come for supper. That way, Mitch, you won't have to busy yourself fixing something to eat the first night you're back."

Several hours later, we were in the kitchen I had conjured up in my mind so many times over the winter. Aromas from pots on the stove mingled with the glow from the fireplace as Marcel uncorked a bottle of homemade sparkling cider. Jeanne served her usual soup of ham bone, cabbage, potatoes, carrots, turnips, onions, leeks, and fresh thyme from her garden, and since it was a special occasion to welcome us back, she added to the pot one of her chickens. She must have slipped a secret ingredient in her cooking because everything she made tasted better than anything I had ever tasted before. As we sat around the table after supper, Roger came by for coffee and Jeanne's *quatre quarts* cake.

"The years haven't done you in yet, Mémé," said Roger, helping himself to a slice. "Yours is still the best *quatre quarts* around."

"That's why I married her," said Marcel, adjusting his glasses.

"Lucky bastard. Smartest thing you ever did," said Jeanne, and poked him with her elbow.

"It's delicious! Would you show me how to make it?" I said.

"Sure will, Mitch. The next time I make it."

"Next to Marcel," said Yves, "that'll make me the luckiest man around." He leaned back, took a drag of his Gauloise cigarette, and looked more relaxed than I'd seen him look in months. Perhaps the tensions of the city had affected us both. Perhaps everything would be different now that we were back in the country.

"Speaking of getting lucky," said Marcel, "you'll never guess which important person drove by and sang out *bonjour* to me this morning."

"Had to be *le curé* from Sulniac," said Roger. "He did me the honor of paying his respects this morning."

"His respects? To either of you?" exclaimed Jeanne, shaking her head. "Why, neither of you has been to church since puberty. Probably came by to lambaste you for that."

"*Dame*, no, Mémé. He had sins worse than that preying on his mind." Roger leaned forward. "Listen. He drives by and parks his car by the side of the field. He squeezes out and lumbers over to the fence, all the time grumbling about his priestly robes dragging in the mud. He motions me over. 'How many children do you have now, my son?' he asks, all of a sudden sounding friendly and paternal as can be. 'Two girls, father,' I answer, just as polite, right back at him. '*Pas plus que ça?*' he says, looking surprised and shaking his head. 'Only *two* after ten years of holy matrimony?' His jowls swing back and forth like they're counting off the years. 'That's all for now, Father,' I say. 'They're growing up just fine.' His face clouds over like somebody just died. He comes close to the fence and leans over the railing. He peers around the empty field to make sure nobody's listening. Then he says, real confidential, 'When a man's been married ten years and there's only two progeny to show for it, I have to ask you, *mon fils*, what have you been doing all these years with your God-given product?' 'Well,' I say to him, 'doing whatever God puts in my head. And, Father, I have to ask you.' I move in closer. 'What do you do with yours?'"

"Merde!" exclaimed Jeanne. "He must think Satan screwed you for sure." She turned to Yves and me. "My boys may not be great believers, but they sure are great blasphemers!" She slapped her knee.

Marcel slid his wire-rimmed glasses down from his nose and wiped them with a handkerchief. "He ought to know better by now than to come 'round here and give advice."

"People used to be afraid to talk back to the priests," said Roger. "Not anymore. Things are changing in the country."

"You're right about that," said Marcel, settling his glasses back on his nose. "Young people are leaving all the time for factory work in the city. Pretty soon there won't be anyone left but old folk to tend the fields."

"Even with our troubles, I'll take a peasant's life any day over a factory worker's," said Roger. "Why would anyone want to move to the city? Pretty soon we'll all have tractors, television—everything."

"Television," Jeanne said with a disdainful wave of her hand. "You'll never get me sitting still for hours staring at a miserable black box."

"You've never seen it, Mémé," Roger said. "Joseph Blevenec bought one for his new house. He says there's singing and dancing and movies on a screen to watch."

Jeanne got up to clear the table. "I'll do my own singing and dancing," she said, snapping her fingers.

"I was in the music business for a while when I wrote the words to songs for Edith Piaf," said Yves.

Everyone turned to him.

"You wrote songs?" asked Roger.

"Just for Piaf. Georges Moustaki was an old friend of mine. He wrote Piaf's music and asked me to come up with lyrics for songs he had written. I still get royalties for them."

Noticing blank expressions on everyone's face, he explained what royalties were and went on to tell how Piaf had survived a troubled childhood, drug addiction, and poverty to become a world-famous singer. They listened politely. Roger helped himself to more cake. Jeanne went to the stove to make another pot of coffee. Marcel rolled a cigarette. Yves and I exchanged glances. Suddenly it was clear that the story, which had always fascinated friends in Paris, had no meaning here. No one knew who Yves had been talking about. They had never heard of Edith Piaf or Georges Moustaki. How could they? They had never seen television, or gone to a movie, or listened to a record player, or watched musicians or singers perform. Their cares and conversations revolved around Blevenec's new tractor, the priest's peculiarities, and Jeanne's *quatre quarts*. Their preoccupations were the shape of a halo around the moon, the weather, the precarious state of planting, and the health of a newborn calf, not celebrities who were famous today and forgotten tomorrow.

How good it was to be back where the ground felt solid under my feet again. No matter what had happened over the past months, La Salle was real and reassuring. It would heal our wounds.

Danielle had started preschool in Paris, and now we needed to find a school for her in the country. All the children from

La Salle and nearly all children from surrounding villages attended the parochial school in Sulniac taught by nuns, most of whom were from nearby farms and villages and hadn't finished basic schooling themselves. Many were superstitious and punctuated their lessons with cautionary tales they themselves had heard as children, stories of wolves and bogeymen lurking behind trees in the woods and ready to pounce on a child who dared talk back to a parent, disobey a teacher, or doubt the Holy Scriptures. Homework wasn't assigned since it was understood that before and after school, children had to help out on the farm. No one expected or prepared them to pursue higher education, and few did. A new law had recently been passed: going to school was now obligatory. Still, many older peasants felt it was a waste of time. For the first time, secular schools were cropping up in villages, although they were poorly attended. The nuns made it clear that anyone who sent their children to those "other schools" had to be either heathens or Communists.

We had heard that the wife of the only other painter in the region, named Jacques Le Brusque, ran a secular school in the living room of their small, cluttered house at the edge of town in Sulniac. Her name was Noël. Normally, there were eight students between the ages of four and fourteen in the school, but three times a year, when a roaming gypsy couple with seven children who traveled around the country in a crowded trailer pulled into Sulniac, the student population swelled to fifteen.

"All the children study together in the same room," Noël explained when we introduced ourselves. "The younger students hear the older ones reciting their lessons. The information gets lodged in their brain so when it's their turn to learn the material, it's familiar stuff to them." A strict, no-nonsense woman and yet affectionate, she held out her arms to embrace Danielle with a hug and kiss. We enrolled Danielle without hesitation and went out to the garage to meet Noël's husband, the painter. Jacques Le Brusque was a slender, slight man with an abundant black moustache and beard. Reciprocally delighted to discover other artists, we spent the rest of the afternoon looking at paintings and exchanging ideas about art and life in the Morbihan.

With Danielle securely in school, we settled back into country life. Off by himself, private, and surrounded by pine woods, Yves threw himself into his work. At last he had the studio of which he had always dreamed. He was also sculpting. On large granite stones framing the doorway of the cider house, where it was now forbidden for me to paint, he chiseled images to represent "Old Man River," a song he loved to hear me sing. One stone was carved to represent me, the singer; others were sculpted into slaves toting that barge or lifting that bale. At either side of the entrance to the courtyard, he drove two huge, heavy wooden posts into the ground and carved his likeness on one and mine on the other. Imposing and proud, they stood guard at the gate and announced to the world the depth of our love for each other.

I kept my sketchbooks out of sight. I hid my oil paints in the cave of the cider house, and by extending trips to the market in Vannes, I was able to sneak in subversive watercolors along the gulf and a small oil landscape from time to time. I didn't mention or show what I was doing to anyone. Often I told myself to rebel, to confront Yves face-to-face and declare that I had in fact been painting in secret, but would no longer submit to such an outrageous dictum. But each time the moment seemed right, I hesitated. We were getting along so well. How could I risk shaking the foundations of my marriage? If Yves was suspicious, he didn't say anything, and we recaptured the harmony that had eluded us over the past months in Paris.

Morning coffee with Jeanne was, by now, a ritual. After dropping Danielle off at school in Sulniac each day, I drove back into the courtyard and saw her signaling me from across the road that coffee was brewing. Her house was the smallest in the village. Like the others, it was built of stone and had a slanted midnight blue slate tile roof. A dirt path in front of the house led to Roger's and Thérèse's farm, and near the fence to the vegetable garden stood a weatherworn, old wooden outhouse. Spilling over the gate to the garden, an immense and fragrant bush of thyme nearly blocked the entrance. Jeanne's vegetable garden was incomparable. Her onions were as large as grapefruits; her cabbages were the size of pumpkins; her tomatoes, carrots, and leeks were the sweetest I had ever tasted; and her shallots were shiny, copper-colored, and aromatic, and stayed firm all year long.

Painted a deep cerulean blue, the door to her house was never locked; locks and keys were unknown in the farmhouses of the Morbihan. Whenever I entered her kitchen, I felt a sense of calm and well-being as never before, and although the floor was pounded dirt, which horrified me at first, her house was immaculate. On the kitchen wall over the long wooden table hung faded old-fashioned family photographs, including one of a younger and thinner Marcel in an army uniform. Next to it was an aging, sepia-tinted

wedding picture of Jeanne with Luc, her first husband, who
stood proudly and stiffly beside her. She was dressed in a
traditional Breton costume, a black dress with colorful em-
broidery down the front and over the sleeves, and her low
lace coif was an especially intricate and beautiful one, the
kind worn only for weddings. Across the room was a wood-
burning stove, and next to it a stone fireplace, where a large
black iron pot sat on an iron grill over flickering embers. A
tiny sink with a cold-water faucet was the only indoor
plumbing. Leaning against a trapdoor in the ceiling, an old,
wooden ladder led to an attic where Jeanne and Marcel slept
on narrow cots. One small window allowed light into the
kitchen. Through lace curtains, it overlooked Jeanne's lush
hydrangea bushes, whose vivid periwinkle blossoms flourished long after others in the village had faded.

Jeanne greeted me at the door cradling a large earthen
bowl in one arm and waving a long, sturdy wooden spoon.
"You're just in time," she said, beaming. "I'm making the
quatre quarts." The ingredients were laid out neatly on the
table: one cup of flour, one cup of sugar, four eggs, and a
pan with four tablespoons of melted butter. "Four equal
parts," she said. "That's why it's called the *quatre quarts*."
She poured the flour and sugar into the bowl and mixed
them. Then she hollowed out a space in the center into
which I cracked the eggs. She mixed the batter again. When
it was smooth, I poured in the melted butter. As she continued stirring, she tilted her head and curved her body around
the bowl so that she and the bowl seemed to fuse and move
as one. As she whipped the batter with the wooden spoon, a
singular expression came over her face, one that I would always think of as Jeanne's *quatre quarts* look. It was a look

of complete absorption and satisfaction; she was focused on the task at hand, and it was one that she did better than anyone else. As she stirred, I added the baking powder and measured a teaspoon of vanilla into the bowl. When the batter was just right—not too thick and not too runny—we arranged apple slices like a fan unfurling around the bottom of a pan she had greased with butter. Continuing to whip the batter, she poured it over the apples, sprinkled sugar over the top, and slipped the pan gently into the oven.

"Now we can have our coffee." She sank down on the bench with a sigh and a contented grin. "We'll smell it when it's done."

Waiting for the *quatre quarts* to bake in her tiny kitchen, as sweet aromas floated through the air, I felt as comfortable and at home as if I had spent my entire childhood growing up in this very place. We talked about many things, whatever came into our minds, and we began to know each other. Listening to her tell me about her life, I felt I had stepped back hundreds of years in time, as if I were sitting across from someone I had known and loved in a distant past, and the thought of it thrilled me.

At two, she was sent to the fields to guard cows that towered over her and at first terrified her, but she did as she was told, and from then on, she never stopped working, not as a child, nor when she married, nor when she had her two sons, was widowed and later remarried, nor as she grew old. The first of six children, she saw her responsibilities multiply with each sibling. When she was eight, her mother died in childbirth. From that moment on, it fell to her to raise her brothers and sisters. Her father was off in the fields, and there was no one else to care for the house or the babies. Like all poor peasants, she never had a childhood. She never went to school and never learned to read or write.

She slapped the table and said matter-of-factly, "Never even learned to write my own name."

"Listen, Jeanne," I said. "I could show you how. In one afternoon, you could write your name. Honestly."

"Too late for that now, Mitch."

"Why? You might need to write your name someday. What if you had to sign a contract?"

"Never will. Marcel does that. But even he doesn't need to sign his name. At the market, when one of us peasants gives our word and shakes on it, it's as good or better than a bunch of scribbles on a scrap of paper."

The cake was done. With a golden brown crust on top, it was soft and moist inside. We let it cool down, flipped it over on a plate, and helped ourselves to a big slice with another cup of coffee. I had never tasted anything like it.

"When you were alone on the farm, Jeanne, did you ever get lonely?" I asked her.

For a moment she was silent. A brief sad expression swept over her face like a passing cloud, but she waved it away with a flick of her wrist and said, "If I did, Mitch, I never put a name to it. Maybe while Luc was a prisoner of those Germans, or after he died and the kids were still young. But Lord knows there's too much work on a farm to dwell on a thing like that."

"How did you and Marcel get together?"

She grinned and took her knitting needles from a basket along with a sweater she was making for Danielle. "It wasn't hard. He was a grouchy old bachelor but didn't put up much of a fight. He lived on a farm two kilometers down the road.

A while after Luc died, he started coming 'round." She tilted her head and smiled coquettishly. "Wasn't much of a surprise to folks when we tied the knot."

I glanced at her wedding photograph on the kitchen wall. She was strong, pretty, and vivacious. Women in the country rarely remarried when they were widowed, but it was no wonder that Jeanne had married again.

"How long did you know Marcel before you married him?"

"How long? Why, I always knew him. I knew both my guys all my life."

"I knew Yves only six months when we married. In the beginning, I could hardly speak French. Trouble began when I began to understand what he was saying." We both laughed.

"What was it that brought you over here, Mitch, all the way from Chicago?" She pronounced it "*Shi*-cago," with the accent on "shi."

"It seems like such a long time ago," I said. "I went to Paris to paint."

"Come to think about it, I haven't seen you painting much lately. Last year, you were always running around picturing."

"I still do, sometimes. But . . . Jeanne, I have to ask you a favor. It sounds crazy, but would it be all right with you and Marcel if I left a few small canvases in a corner of your stable? They would hardly take up any room."

"*Dame, sûr.* You can keep as many as you like over here. But why, Mitch? Seems to me you've got seven houses to put them in."

"I know it sounds silly. It's just that Yves doesn't like it when I paint. I have to hide the paintings."

"We'll put them in a box on the shelf with the chickens. They'll be safe there." She put down her knitting and frowned. "But painting pictures is what you do. Didn't you once tell me you always did it, even when you were little?"

"I can't remember when I didn't paint. But he feels too strongly about it."

"It's not right. No one ought to clip the wings off a bird." She frowned and shook her head. "So you went to Paris to paint. Did you know people there?"

"I didn't know anyone. Not a soul."

She pushed aside the knitting basket. "I don't know which of us is crazier." She clasped my hand in hers. "You running around the world like a chicken with its head cut off or me, sitting in one place like a hen with its backside glued to the nest. However you got here"—she tightened her grasp on my hand—"it's good you found your way to La Salle!"

11

The Muse

"Poor Grande Moustache," I said, telling her about Yves' cat. "The day we married, she ran away. She must have sensed a new mistress had taken over the house."

"Cats know everything," said Jeanne, nodding in agreement.

"As long as I was Yves' girlfriend, she tolerated me," I went on. "She was always a little crazy, but when my family arrived for the wedding and she saw me move in with my suitcases, she acted more demented than ever. The finishing touch was the wedding party. All evening long, she crouched like a cornered tigress under the table in Yves' studio; her eyes darted back and forth like fiery searchlights in the night. She couldn't stand to see all those people laughing, drinking champagne, and toasting to Yves' and my happiness. Poor thing. She must have been heartbroken. That night, while no one paid attention, she sneaked out the door. She scampered down six flights of stairs and disappeared in the night. At first we were sure she'd come back. She'd gone prowling

before, and after a few days she'd always reappear, covered
with war scars and unrepentant. Not this time. Weeks went
by. We made sketches of her and tacked them in shops and
on tree trunks around the neighborhood. No luck. We looked
for her for months and months, but we never found her. I
hate to think what might have happened."

"Cats run off, but they come back when they get hungry
enough."

"Maybe in the country. But a city is filled with danger
for a cat. She could have been run over by a car or a bus. She
could have lost her way, or someone could have stolen her.
But the worst was when Yves' landlady told me that an Italian family in our neighborhood loved cat meat. Oh, God. I
just hope that Grande Moustache didn't end up in one of
their pasta sauces."

"Did you really think they got her and chopped her up?"

"No, no! Of course not." The idea was so frightful we
couldn't help laughing, groaning, and hugging each other at
the same time. "Besides," I said, brushing aside a tear, "I
never believed the landlady. She was a terrible gossip. And
even if the Italian family had tried to catch her, Grande
Moustache would have outsmarted them. She was the craft-
iest cat I ever knew. I'll bet she snuggled up to someone nice
on the street who picked her up and gave her a good home.
Probably another painter. Or maybe a writer. She was an
artist's cat. Sometimes I think she really was a muse."

"What's that?"

"Someone who gives an artist inspiration or an idea,
when he can't think of what to do next."

"Anyway, seems to me a cat is better off in the country."
Jeanne grabbed a stick leaning against the wall and poked at

logs in the fireplace until the fire crackled and the logs sent sparks flying up the chimney chute. "What's it like, Mitch, living in a big city like Paris?" she asked, coming over to the table and sitting on the bench across from me.

"I loved it from the minute I set foot in it," I said. I told her how the first day I arrived, I rented a room on the sixth floor of a cheap hotel on the Left Bank of the river Seine.

She squinted at me skeptically. "Six floors? That sounds more far-fetched than one of my tall tales."

"Honestly," I said, "the hotel was six stories high and my room was on the top. There was one narrow window that overlooked the rooftops of the city, and the bathroom was down the hall."

All her life she had had only an outhouse; indoor plumbing of any kind was unknown to her. After explaining what a bellboy was, I told her how I asked the hotel desk clerk for permission to paint in the room, and almost immediately, a frail elderly white-haired bellboy appeared at the door with tattered blankets that he tacked to the walls to protect them from the dripping and splashing of paint. When I told her that one day I would take her to Paris, she laughed and shrugged. "What would an old peasant woman like me do in a big city?"

I described tall buildings with elevators and tree-lined boulevards with traffic speeding in both directions, the high-pitched honking of small cars jostling for position in narrow streets, and the endless parade of entwined couples strolling along the banks of the Seine.

"How did you and Yves get together?" she asked. She got up and brought a bottle of cider to the table and filled glasses for both of us.

I told her about going to the opening of Le Guerrec's art show, and how I had noticed Yves right away in the art gallery. I told her how he invited me to his studio to see his work, and how I loved his paintings. I told her everything— well, not quite everything. I left out certain things. For instance, I didn't mention that we made love or lived together before we married. She was from another culture and a different generation; I didn't want to shock her. But I did tell her how much I loved him, and although she never said so, judging from the gentle, teasing way they were with each other and the sly, affectionate looks they exchanged, it was clear that Jeanne and Marcel cared for each other, too. I asked her what qualities she thought were important in a husband. Without hesitation she answered, "A man who isn't mean and who is a hard worker."

Exactly what my grandmother used to tell me, I thought, smiling to myself.

"Of course, in the beginning," I said, "I didn't speak French too well. Yves and I could hardly understand each other. Just like I couldn't understand you at first."

"And like it was for me and my boys," Jeanne said as we walked to her vegetable garden to uproot a cabbage for supper. "Gallo was all I spoke until they went to school and had to speak French."

"Roger and Marcel spoke Gallo when they were little, didn't they?"

"Sure. But if they spoke it in school, they got punished by having to wear a wooden sabot tied around their neck. They had to wear it until the next poor kid slipped and said a word in Gallo."

"To humiliate them?"

"*Dame, oui.* Everyone made fun of the guy wearing the sabot. In no time, they were all speaking only French. At first, half the time I didn't know what the devil they were talking about."

"Do you know how smart you are?" I said, shutting the gate to the garden behind us. "You've never been to school and still you speak two languages."

"God knows how many I'd speak if I'd gone to school," she said with a wink.

"Teach me words in Gallo," I said.

"Let's see. *Demad.* That means *bonjour.*"

"*De-mad.*"

"*Kenavo.*"

"*Kenavo,*" I repeated.

"That means *au revoir. Garçon.* In Gallo, that's *paotr.*"

"*Pa-oh* . . . That's a hard one," I said. "I love trying to pronounce them!"

She laughed. "You and I will be chatting together in Gallo in no time." She thrust her spade under a cabbage. Flicking her fingers, she tapped the soil off the roots and wrapped her apron around it. She broke off a sprig of thyme from the enormous bush by the fence, and we headed back to the kitchen.

"So when Danielle came along, you and Yves decided to buy a place in the country?"

"We were looking for a small, easy-to-manage farmhouse. I still can't believe we bought half of a hamlet."

"When people around here heard city folks were buying up Blevenec's old farm, they thought those folks must be crazy."

"Just wait. Once we fix up these old farmhouses and they see how comfortable they can be, they'll change their minds."

Yet, even as I spoke, I understood why the peasants thought we were crazy. The timeworn dwellings were painful reminders of a harsh past, a life they longed to escape and put behind them. A stable and pigsty might be worth keeping for cows and pigs, but why would any sane person spend money on these relics for living quarters when they could raze them to the ground and make room for one of the modern, semi-prefabricated houses that came in three varieties and could be seen multiplying all over the region like rabbits let loose from a cage. Dorso and Company, a demolition establishment from Theix, was busy around the countryside with a bulldozer, wrecking old farms with a Savonarola-like fervor as if they were a satanic blight on the landscape. The owner, Dorso himself, was the closest I had ever seen to a French version of a redneck. His swollen belly spilled over his belt, the back of his neck bulged over his shirt, and an air of vulgarity about him mirrored the crushing and disemboweling maneuvers of his bulldozer. Embodying everything that threatened the pristine beauty of the Morbihan, in a matter of hours, without pity or remorse, he succeeded in smashing timeless old farms and trees that had served well for centuries. For a fraction of the money the peasants spent demolishing their graceful old dwellings with slanted slate roofs and yard-thick granite walls, they could install modern comforts in the old farmhouses and preserve the memories entombed within them. And put Dorso and Company out of business.

It amazed me that, from the beginning, Yves had recognized the potential of La Salle. I became aware of it the day the rambling old warehouse was dismantled when, as if by magic, an unobstructed view all the way to the sea was unveiled. Getting to feel at ease with the neighbors and watching Danielle thrive and nestle snugly into country life fueled my growing attachment to the hamlet. But it was the affection I had come to feel for Jeanne that sealed my conversion. Yves was probably right. Maybe I would always be a city person, an outsider to her; and as he often reminded me, she and I had nothing in common. Yet I loved being with her more than with most people I had ever known. I couldn't explain it even to myself, but when I was with her I felt safe, as if she would protect me from anything that might harm me. More and more, I felt as if I were a part of La Salle, like a transplanted tree whose roots were gradually inching and embedding their way into the ground around them.

Work on the houses was going well, and I enjoyed working with the masons and carpenters from Frères Calaix. But it was hard to endure watching Yves go briskly to his studio in the mornings, serving him coffee at his breaks, listening to him talk about the problems in his work, the obstacles, breakthroughs, joys, and triumphs of each canvas. I found it harder and harder to sneak away for painting excursions and threw myself into the mushrooming job of restoring La Salle, as if it might fill the void inside me. Each day was consuming more of my energies, as if a giant spider had ensnared me and had drawn me deeper and deeper into its bottomless web. More material than expected was needed, more decisions had to be made, more expenses than we had counted on cropped up. In the evenings, while Yves made sketches of paintings he would work on the following day, I spent hours figuring how to survive the rising costs. Reluctantly, I wrote my father to ask for a loan to help with spiraling expenses. He answered, saying he would send the money and consider it a belated birthday present for Danielle. He said one day he would come to see La Salle. I wrote back a long letter with detailed sketches of each house, a drawing to scale of the layout of the land, and told him how grateful we were to him. I wrote him that for now, we were still in temporary quarters while the main house was overrun by workmen dismantling, scraping, constructing, installing, hammering, and painting. Once the work was finished, we would love for him to visit. Then he would see for himself it truly was a good investment. Half the hamlet was ours, I wrote, and soon a country house one could only dream about would be a reality.

12

Stormy Weather

As THE HAY ABOUT TO BE HARVESTED lay strewn over the fields, the sky turned dark without warning. Heavy steel-colored clouds appeared from nowhere and swept across the sky. Thunder rumbled in the distance. Across the road, Jeanne and Marcel rushed from their house and ran toward the fields. Yves burst out of his studio. I called to him, "What's wrong?"

"Rain!" he shouted back. "It could ruin the hay." He ran after Jeanne and Marcel. Having spent boyhood summers on a family farm in Auvergne when he used to help the farmers, Yves knew exactly what the crisis was about. If the hay drying on the field got drenched, there would be no hay to feed the cows and pigs the following year. Time was crucial. The hay had to be lifted and piled into steep, firmly packed cone-shaped mounds so that when the rain came, it would dampen and damage only the outer layers. Although I still didn't understand what was happening, obviously it was a crisis. I took Danielle's hand and ran to Roger's and Thérèse's house and left her with Jacqueline. An unnatural wind rustled the pine trees on the hill above. Behind the house, a narrow path bordered by thick, thorny briars led to the fields. I fought through branches whipped by the wind, crisscrossing, lashing, blocking my way. When finally I forced my way to a clearing, I could see the villagers clustered together at the far end of the field. Yves was pitching hay along with the rest of them. A streak of sunlight pierced through the clouds, illuminating them like one of Yves' bucolic paintings of peasants gathered in a sunlit field. A moment later, clouds converged and engulfed the scene in darkness, transforming the villagers into anguished Munchian figures.

Everyone was working feverishly. Lifting the hay appeared to be strenuous, but I was sure I could do it too. I grabbed an idle pitchfork leaning against a tree, loaded it awkwardly, and threw the hay onto one of the mounds, imitating their motion but leaving a straggling trail of hay behind. The pitchfork was harder to manipulate than I thought. Yves laughed and called out, "Look everyone! My American wants to be a *paysanne*!"

Jeanne lay her pitchfork on a mound of hay and came over beside me. "Watch, Mitch. Plant your legs apart like this. You're more balanced that way. Grab the handle with one hand at the top and the other close to the fork so you can twist it when you lift the hay."

I tried. It seemed to work better. I tried again. She stood watching me with her hands on her hips. "*C'est bien*, Mitch. That's it!" She turned to the others and shouted, "She's got the knack now."

I worked alongside them throughout the day until late in the afternoon when the rain erupted and pummeled the ground. Soaked through and exhausted, we ran for cover under a wooden shed at the far end of the field and waited for the rain to stop. After thirty minutes the storm cleared. Everyone came out into the open to assess the damage and poked at the stacks to see how deep the downpour had penetrated. Since most of the hay had been piled into mounds before the rains came crashing down, loss had been held to a minimum. The hay would have to remain untouched until the sun dried the outer layers, but enough had been rescued to feed the animals the following year. Disaster had been averted.

"You were a real help, Mitch," Jeanne said afterward, hugging me.

The palms of my hands were covered with blisters, and my back ached so badly it was painful to stand upright, but I didn't mind. I felt even closer to Jeanne, and from then on, the villagers treated me differently. I was no longer a foreigner.

Several days later, I went to Jeanne's house to get our usual supply of eggs. No one was in the kitchen. "Jeanne! It's Midge," I called out. There was no answer. I crossed the corridor and opened the door to the small barn, which was just large enough to crowd three cows on one side and squeeze the chickens along the other. Through the door, I saw her leaning against a wooden post. Her face was pale and distorted with pain. She leaned on me as I helped her from the stable into the kitchen.

"It's my liver, Mitch. The doctor said so." Her voice was breathy and weak. "Roger went to fetch him. He came yesterday. I told him I fell against the side of the barn while I was milking Moomoot."

"You fell?"

"Well, Moomoot might have given me a shove or two to help me along." She managed to wink.

"Wait a minute. Moomoot kicked and you fell. So how could it be your liver?"

"Dr. Gavin said that's what it was. I'll just rest here a while."

Dr. Gavin! That explained it. It was said he often remarked how curious it was that so many patients died under his care. Of course he wasn't the only doctor in France to judge every illness, no matter how disparate, to be a liver ailment. But Jeanne had fallen against a cement wall, and was in far too much pain to dismiss it as *mal au foie*. I tried to make her comfortable and drove to Vannes to get Dr. Le Cam, our family doctor. He was at home and followed me back to La Salle. Nothing was wrong with her liver. Moomoot had kicked over her stool. She had fallen and had fractured several ribs. Dr. Le Cam wrote out a prescription for pain and gave me instructions for applying compresses. For the next week, Jeanne allowed herself to be my patient. Usually briskly independent, she didn't protest. It seemed she enjoyed being pampered.

"Remember when I first came to La Salle and was afraid of cows?" I teased as I applied a cold compress. "You see? I was right! I knew from the start they were dangerous."

"It wasn't Moomoot's fault, Mitch. She kicked, but I fell on my own."

Caring for her, I became increasingly aware how difficult her life was and how it had become even more harsh for her as she grew older. So that she wouldn't have to climb a ladder at night, Marcel and I brought her cot down from the attic to the kitchen, where she would sleep until her ribs healed. She had only a backless wooden bench to sit on. The next afternoon, I drove to Vannes and bought her a wicker armchair with cushions so she could lean back and rest on them. It was the first comfortable chair she had ever sat in. Watching her slide into it, snuggle back against the cushions, and pick up her knitting with a contented sigh gave me more pleasure than I could describe. To heat water, she had to fill a heavy iron pot with cold water and drag it from the sink to the fireplace. I added a gas-powered water heater to my shopping list of things to buy for her as soon as I could save the money. While she was recuperating, we spent more and more time together, sitting at her kitchen table and talking over coffee or a glass of cider. As her pain subsided, she began calling me the daughter she never had.

"Tell me about Luc," I said to her one day.

"Luc Diquero? *Eh, bien, ma fille,* what can I say? He wasn't a bad guy, except for his drinking."

She went on to tell me that when the Second World War broke out, nearly all the young men in the countryside were conscripted into the army. Too old to fight, Luc remained at La Salle until he was captured by German soldiers as they swept through the villages and, except for young boys, the sick, and the elderly, rounded up the men as prisoners of war. Luc was taken to a farm labor camp in the south of Germany. The villages were depleted of men, and for the women who stayed behind, raising children; caring for cows, chickens, pigs, goats; and planting and harvesting the crops without a man's help, life was at least as hard as what many of the soldiers and prisoners endured.

"Sure it wasn't easy with the farm and two kids," she

said, shrugging. "But Luc, poor devil. Those Germans held him for nearly four years. It could have been worse. The man who ran the farm wasn't mean, and Luc did the same thing he'd been doing all his life, working the fields all day and sleeping on a hard cot at night. He went hungry sometimes, but being on a farm, there was always something he could scrounge around for. His farmer grew oats. There were days he lived on raw oats, like a horse. Said it saved him. And he had beer. All he could drink. It's the beer that killed him, Mitch. When the war was over, he came home but his health was gone. People said he was drinking himself into a grave. A year later, he was dead."

"So you were alone again on the farm."

"Just till I latched onto Marcel." She winked impishly.

"What was Marcel like back then?"

"Him? Same as now. He never changes. He's always got a sweet disposition. He's the gentlest man on God's earth. Why, he can't even kill a chicken!"

"Yves says everyone in the country can kill a chicken. I could never do it. But he says if I eat them, I have to kill them."

"That's not so. Most often there's one person on a farm who does the killing. Between me and Marcel, I do it. Not that I get pleasure from it, like some folks, but I don't mind. Not him. Kill a chicken? Why, he can't even watch while I pluck it! When his dog got hit by a car coming up the hill and I had to put it out of its misery, he broke down and cried like a baby. Couldn't talk about it for weeks without him crying. Marcel couldn't drown a litter of cats even if a farm is flooded with them. I have to do that. There isn't a mean bone in his body. Even when he drinks too much. He never changes."

Jeanne loved telling stories about her mother. Once she told me how strong her mother was. "Listen. All by herself, she'd lift a wooden cabinet that four husky men couldn't budge. Merde, she was tougher than any guy. She was as strong as a bear and afraid of nothing. She could jump on a horse while it was galloping at full speed. She'd snatch the reins on the run, grab the saddle, and swing herself right onto the horse's back without his even slowing down. It was a sight!"

"Like a champion rodeo rider from the West," I said, applauding and explaining who the rodeo riders were.

"She would have beat 'em all," she said, beaming.

She remembered how her mother prepared food for her father, six siblings, and day workers at midday and evening supper, often for ten or more people. Her mother never sat down at the table, but stood close to the stove, holding her plate as she ate, overseeing a meal of potatoes, cabbage soup, and huge loaves of bread she had baked herself. She tended a garden, cured meats for the winter, raised the children, and worked in the fields alongside the men.

"I never dreamed a woman had to work so hard," I said.

"Not only that, but she was working in the potato fields the day before each of her babies was born and was back in the fields the next afternoon. And then she died young— giving birth. It was a boy. He would have been her seventh child. They both died. I remember that, too."

"You were only eight. And you had to take over and do all the work your mother had done."

"There was no one else to do it. And we didn't have electricity or running water in the house," Jeanne added with a smile that deepened the lines carved into her face. "We only got them a few years ago. It's easier for women now." Her eyes shone, and behind the worn and weather-beaten exterior I could see the face of the proud young peasant bride in the yellowing photograph on the kitchen wall.

Before Jeanne's accident with Moomoot, she had seen a doctor only once, years ago, when she was in her early thirties. She had become seriously ill, and her family summoned Dr. Le Bec from the nearby town of Musillac. After a drawn-out examination, he informed the family that her condition was grave and took her off in the night to a clinic run by the sisters. She got worse. After a few days, she was on her deathbed. The black-robed sisters stood grim-faced around her.

"Jeanne Diquero," one of the nuns said somberly, "at most, you have a week to live. Do you want to die here at the clinic or take your last breath at home on the farm? It's your choice, my child."

". . . At home, *ma sœur,*" Jeanne said feebly.

Back at La Salle, her two small sons, Roger and Marcel; her husband, Luc; and her family and neighbors hovered around her bed and tearfully asked if she had any last requests. She struggled to speak. Someone leaned close to her mouth. *"Un verre de cidre,"* she whispered, barely audibly. Holding her head, they brought a glass of cider to her lips. She managed a sip, then another, then limply motioned for another glass. After a few more sips, she raised her head and tried to sit up. The next glass she held by herself, and color began flowing back into her chalk white face. She started looking more and more like herself every minute, her body functioned again, and after a week, she was up and around the house, fully recovered. She vowed to stay away from the sisters and never to see a doctor as long as she lived.

Thirty years went by, and Dr. Le Bec never had occasion to return to the village. Then one day, Roger brought the old doctor to La Salle to examine Claudine, who had come down with an unidentifiable childhood illness. As Roger walked with him past Jeanne's house, the doctor shook his head sadly and pointed with his cane.

"*Eh, oui*, I remember. That's the farm where your poor mother, Jeanne Diquero, used to live," he said, his voice quaking with emotion. "It broke my heart to see you two little guys lose your young mother. I never got over it when she passed on," he sighed, brushing aside a tear rolling down his cheek.

"Don't be upset, Dr. Le Bec. Mémé's still here. Same house as always," said Roger.

"Eh? What's that? Still here?"

"That's right."

"She can't be . . ."

"She remarried. She's Jeanne Montrelay now."

"But she died."

"No, Dr. Le Bec. She's still here. Doing fine."

"She died forty years ago!"

"She didn't die."

"She died, *she died!*"

Jeanne told the story with relish. "All those years, the good doctor mourned my passing," she said, laughing and slapping her thigh. "For forty years, no one bothered to tell him I was still around. Poor Dr. Le Bec. He never got over the shock."

One afternoon, late that summer, I went with Yves to the garage where he kept his machete to trim the thornbushes. As he reached for it hanging on a hook, he caught sight of a small canvas I had been working on in secret. It was an oil painting of a path leading to an old farmhouse, shaded by a huge oak tree and painted in tones of blues and umber. I had hidden it behind boxes, had carelessly left a corner of it partially uncovered because it was still wet, and planned to sneak it to Jeanne's stable as soon as it was dry. Furious, he grabbed it, struck it with the machete, and slit it in two. From the entrance of the garage, dumbfounded, I watched as he walked impassively in front of me and over to the wooden post at the entrance to the courtyard, the one on which he had sculpted my likeness. With the machete still in hand and with a ferocious crack of his wrist, he slashed off a part of my double's chin.

For the rest of the day, I couldn't speak to him. Or look at him. That night, I didn't sleep. At three in the morning, I crept out of bed, threw on an overcoat, grabbed my clandestine box of watercolors, and drove off in the night. Driving around the countryside, I saw two cows grazing peacefully on a hillside in the moonlight. I parked the car off the road and wriggled under a fence. As the morning light filtered through the night sky, I set out my watercolors and began to paint while the cows grazed nearby, indifferent to my presence. Dawn unfolded with delicate mauves, beiges, and pale yellows, blending like actors gliding soundlessly across a stage. By the time the sun had risen, my watercolor was finished. I packed up my paints and headed back to La Salle. Returning through the entrance to the courtyard, I passed

117

by the wooden post with the gash across my double's chin and shuddered. For a moment, I thought I saw blood gushing like white water from the wound.

There was no sign of life on our side of the road, but I knew Jeanne would be awake.

"Mitch. Where are you going at this time of day?" she said.

"I went for a drive. I saw some cows in a meadow, Jeanne. How can they be so tranquil? We take their milk, rob them of their calves, and butcher them for beef stew. Why don't they rebel? Why don't they save themselves and run away?"

She put her hand on my shoulder and tilted her head to one side. "What's wrong, *ma fille*?"

"Listen. I have to get Danielle ready for school. When I get back, I'm going to the beach. Please, will you come with me?"

"You know I've never been to the water."

"Well, this is a perfect day to see it for the first time. Will you come?"

"Marcel," she called inside. "Mitch and I are going to the beach."

"You sure about that, Mémé?" He continued drinking his coffee. Then he looked up and said wryly, "Have a nice swim, both of you."

⌒

One of the few times I ever saw Jeanne frightened was when we arrived at the sea. She hesitated getting out of the car, so we sat there for a while, watching the waves sweep over the beach and rhythmically withdraw.

"You're going into that water?" she asked incredulously.

I nodded. "Whenever you're ready, we can go on the beach."

Uneasy when her feet sank into the sand, she clutched my arm as we made our way to the shore. The water was still high for me to swim; the tide wouldn't be going out for another hour. I had worn a bikini under my shorts. I slipped off the shorts and dropped them onto the sand.

"Mitch! What are you doing taking off your clothes? You'll catch your death!" Her face was pale and tense.

"It's all right," I said, laughing. "I have my bathing suit on."

Since Jeanne had never seen a bathing suit, my scant bikini wasn't much reassurance. "You look naked to me," she said with a look of concern.

"This is what people wear to go swimming. Honestly. Wait here. I'm going in. I won't be long."

I threw myself into the water. Not only had Jeanne never seen the sea, she had never seen anyone in it. I began swimming, then treaded water and looked back at her. She was standing rigidly at the water's edge, holding on to her coif, her black dress flapping in the wind. I waved. She waved back, and then I turned toward the horizon. On the crest of a wave, I swam out to sea. I felt I could swim forever, but a wave crashed over me as if to remind me that no matter how far out to sea I might swim, I still had to go back and face the storm swirling around Yves and me like a whirlpool sucking us under, each day becoming more and more ominous, threatening to engulf us. I tasted the saltiness of the waves. My arms seemed to be self-propelling, as if they didn't belong to me. Leaving floods of tears behind me, I let myself be carried along by the peaks and valleys of the waves and swam and swam until I could barely see the shore. I lost track of time. Then, suddenly, Jeanne's image flashed across my mind. She was standing on the beach, anxiously looking out over the waves, searching for me. I turned to swim back to shore. When I pulled myself out, exhilarated and dripping, she was standing at the edge of the water, her face ashen with fear.

"Mitch!" she managed to say.

"You didn't need to worry, you know," I said. "I'm a good swimmer."

"I never saw anything like it in my whole life," she said, catching her breath and wrapping a towel around me. "You went out so far. I couldn't see you. The water must be over your head!"

I described to her what it was like being in deep water and the feeling of the sea closing around me, how it released all the tension churning inside of me; how lying on my back and letting myself be rocked and tossed by the waves made me feel limp, light-headed, like a grain of sand cast about in a huge ocean.

"Mitch," she sighed. "I didn't understand a single word."

"Someday I'll take you for a swim, and you'll see for yourself," I said, sliding my arm through hers.

We sat on a rock to watch the waves. The tide was slowly and gently easing its way out. I persuaded her to take off her shoes and stockings, and we walked to the water's edge. She held up her skirt and ventured in to where the water was at our ankles; we stood there for a while, feeling the insistent pull of the tide underneath our feet. Her fear seemed to evaporate as she splashed her feet in the shallow pools of water and watched the sand seep through her toes. Walking along the shore, we were an odd pair, she in her lace coif and long, billowing black skirt and me in my bikini. The beach had always fascinated me when the tide was out, but sharing the experience with her made it more thrilling, more intense, like watching a child at the seashore for the first time. The feel of the sand, the splash of a wave, the sight of pebbles and shells washed up on the shore, the salty smell of the sea breeze—everything was fresh and exciting.

As the sea withdrew, a completely new seascape emerged. Our toes dug into a different texture of sand, one that had been submerged, unexposed to air or sunlight. Left-behind puddles of seawater harbored strange creatures whose existence had remained unknown as long as the tide was in. Nervous crabs darted in and out of the muddy sand. Under rocks, clusters of mussels clung with their life force. We yanked them from their hiding places and threw them into her apron, which she had knotted together to contain our plunder. "Lunch," she said, grinning, rattling them together. We watched as other creatures ventured from the depths for a brief moment in the light. We passed sparse figures dressed in black who dotted the lonely beach, hovering over the sand with their buckets and nets, intently focused on the unseen, ready to pounce on the slightest sign of life stirring in the seafloor, eager to pluck the hidden, secretive, edible treasures from the sea. Finally, we walked back to the rock where we had left our clothes and shoes. Hours later, after we had gone, the sea would return on schedule, gradually, gently, like a blanket being drawn over a sleeping child.

13

Genie out of the Box

RAIN WAS COMING DOWN IN TORRENTS. I left the doctor's office and hailed a passing taxi.

"Where to?" he growled. The storm had caused a hopeless tie-up in traffic. A stoplight turned from red to green over and over, and we couldn't budge from the intersection of avenue de l'Opéra and rue de Rivoli. Fragments of the conversation I had with the doctor throbbed in my head like magnified echoes of my heartbeat. "Cyclic personality . . . that's the medical term for it . . . all his life . . . without medication . . . only get worse . . . moments of calm, spiraling into violence . . ." The words wouldn't stop. They kept repeating, "Cyclic personality . . . without medication, would never be under control . . ." He was sick. If he would not take medication, his sickness would never be under control. Rain was pounding against the car. The windows were steaming. I was in a cage. My throat tightened. I wanted to scream.

"You all right?"

Startled, I looked up and saw the driver eyeing me in the rearview mirror. Thrusting a massive arm over the front seat, he swiveled around to face me. A shiny, purplish scar zigzagged across his forehead. Heavyset, swarthy, and menacing, he looked like an escaped convict.

"The minute you got in my cab, I knew it," he said in a gravelly voice.

"Knew what?"

"Something's wrong, isn't it?"

I sat up straight. "Excuse me?"

"You're afraid to go home. Is that it?"

Tears were welling up in my eyes, and I rummaged through my bag for a Kleenex.

"It's your husband, right?"

"Pardon me?"

"I can tell. It's your husband."

"Certainly not!" I found a handkerchief and blew my nose. I looked at him again. Until that moment, I had spoken to no one. I couldn't talk to friends; they were *his* friends. I couldn't talk to family; it was *his* family. Certainly I couldn't tell my troubles to Danielle. She was his daughter, too, and she was only five! My family was far away in Chicago, and besides, they were so fond of him. Even if I were to tell them, what could they do to help? Run home to Chicago? It was out of the question. How could I go back? How could I take Danielle that far from her father? Besides, France was my home now. But I was alone. There was no one I could confide in.

"What's wrong?" he said in a gruff voice that sounded

like an order. So to this man whom I had never seen before, I told everything.

⁓

Since the day Yves found my painting at La Salle, he had changed drastically. The man I loved and thought I knew had mutated into someone rigid and frightening from whom I felt estranged, leaving me bewildered, as if I were stumbling on quicksand with nothing to grab onto to regain my footing. Then suddenly he would be himself again—but was he? A minute later, without warning, his mood would shift and he would fly into a fit of anger. At first, those moments were rare, and he was remorseful afterward. Then they became more frequent, more virulent, and soon they were happening every day, all the time, upon awakening in the morning, in the afternoon, in the middle of the night, without reason. One morning, he was in his studio going through the usual bills and notices that arrived in the morning mail. I heard him roar "Merde *alors*!" He threw the letters to the floor and stormed into the kitchen where I was cleaning up after lunch. "They'll never be satisfied until they have my money, my house, everything! Well, they can go to hell!" He yanked a plate from my hand and threw it against the wall.

"Yves, what's gotten into you?" I said, staring at the shattered plate on the floor. "That's our dinner plate!"

"It was? Well then, they can take this, the bastards!" He grabbed a kitchen chair, slammed it against the wall, stomped on it, and smashed it to pieces. Watching him, I felt numb. I didn't recognize him. His face was transformed: his eyes were half closed, his cheeks flushed, and his mouth drawn back into a grimace I'd never seen before. Abruptly he turned, went back into his studio, and slammed the door. I sat down at the kitchen table and cried. My tears were partly from fright, partly from concern. What was happening to him? What could I do? I used to think the love we felt for each other would calm his anxieties. But not anymore. I wiped my tears, took a broom, and swept up the pieces from the kitchen floor.

Several days later, Yves went out on an errand in the afternoon and didn't return home until late that night. I was getting ready for bed.

"Where have you been? I was worried."

"Don't lie to me," he said in an agitated voice.

"Lie to you?"

"*Putain!* Whore! I know what's been going on. You've been sleeping around!"

"Don't talk to me that way! You know that's not true."

"Lies, Maude. Lies, lies!"

"Yves, Maude is your mother, not me."

"I know who you are!" he shouted and pounded his fist through the wall. I could hear Danielle in the next room, crying. I ran to reassure her. I promised her it was a bad dream. After she had gone back to sleep, I got the broom and swept up the plaster from the floor. It seemed that was all I was doing those days.

⌒

The taxi driver was silent, as if waiting for me to go on. Then he whipped around. "And now he's turned on you. Right?"

I didn't answer.

"Listen. Once a man crosses that line, he never comes back."

"Never?" I gasped.

"Never."

"But that can't be. I just came from seeing our doctor. He said if he'd agree to take medication, in time—"

"Once the genie is out of the box, it only gets worse."

"Oh, God. That's what the doctor said. 'It will only get worse.' But why? What did I do?"

"It's got nothing to do with you," he said unequivocally. "You've got to know that. It's his problem."

"What do you mean?"

"He's afraid he's losing his virility."

"Oh, it couldn't be that."

"Listen. When a man fears for his manhood, he blames a woman, flies into a rage, and beats her up. That way, it's not his fault, it's hers."

"But he is sure of himself in that way. He's strong. He was a boxer at art school. He's a beautiful man."

I must have sounded foolish. "He's not sure of himself when he's beating you," he said.

As if a flood of emotion dammed up inside me had broken loose, nothing could hold it back now. "He hasn't wanted to make love for a long time," I said. Although shocked at revealing something so intimate to a stranger, I couldn't stop. "He was always so loving, so passionate. Now all he does is lie on the sofa in his studio, staring into space. He won't see a doctor. If I mention it, he flies into a rage. He doesn't want me to go outside, except to do the marketing or take our daughter to school. I lied today to see the doctor. I'm in prison. It gets worse every day."

I told him about Danielle, and how our five-year-old was hearing and witnessing things a child should never see. My fears about what this might do to her eclipsed fears I might have had for myself. That morning, I walked her to school. When I kissed her goodbye outside the schoolhouse, she said, "Come to school with me, Mommy. Show the teacher where it hurts." She reached up to touch the bruise on my forehead and gently patted the bandage on my arm. "She'll make it well."

Walking home from school, I passed a gendarme on the sidewalk. He smiled, tipped his hat, and said, *"Bonjour, mademoiselle."*

I wanted to grab his arm and tell him what was happening. I wanted to tell him my husband had hurt me the night before. I wanted to tell him I was afraid to go home. But I couldn't. I turned and hurried home—to Yves.

For a long time, I went on talking to the taxi driver. He listened as I poured out my feelings and fears, and when he answered, he was wise and understanding. After a while, I glanced out the window. "Oh, God. We're home! I didn't realize. I have to go in. I'm very late now. He'll be furious."

"Look," he said gently. "You don't want to admit it, but you know you're in danger."

"Yes. I know."

"You're young and strong. You've got to show him you're strong." He looked directly at me. "You want me to go up with you?"

I looked into his eyes, and they seemed kind to me now. Even the scar across his forehead looked benign and reassuring. He meant it. He would have come upstairs with me to confront Yves.

"I'm okay," I said. "But thank you. For everything."

He held out a coarse, enormous hand to me. I grasped it, hoping some of his strength and confidence would seep into mine. He waited while I walked to the entrance, and I waved back at him as I went inside. In the elevator, I wondered how Yves would have reacted if a brawny, scar-faced bodyguard had escorted me home. A missed opportunity, I mused, and put the key in the door.

⌒

"We have to talk," I said.

As if sedated, Yves was stretched out on the sofa in his studio. No canvas was on the easel. There was no evidence of any work in progress.

"If you want to talk about last night, forget it," he said in a weary voice. "It was your fault. You drive me to it."

"Yves, last night was not my fault. I've brought tea. We need to talk." I handed him a cup and poured his tea. "I've been thinking about what's been happening to us. You need an atmosphere where you can get back to your painting. You need to be alone for a while."

"What are you talking about? I have a wife and a kid. How can I be alone?"

"You have to be. I've decided to take Danielle to La Salle for a few months."

"That's crazy." Life had come back into his voice. "It's winter. You'd both freeze to death."

"There's a fireplace. I'll build fires."

"Forget it. You don't know how to build a fire. Besides, you belong here. You can't take Danielle out of school in the middle of the year."

"Noël will give her special attention. She'll be fine. We have to separate for a while. I know it and you know it, too."

"You're out of your mind. You're from a big city. You could never handle La Salle on your own. Not in the summer and certainly not in the middle of winter. And what about me? Do you think you can you just run off and leave your responsibilities while you go off on some idiotic idea?"

"I'll take the camionette," I said. "You'll have the Deux Chevaux. I'm going to pack a few things now. We'll leave first thing tomorrow morning."

He stared straight ahead. His eyes again seemed lifeless. All the fire and vitality had gone out of them.

───⌒───

It was windy and damp that January morning when Yves helped bring the boxes and suitcases to the car.

"Be a good girl, Poucette," he said tenderly to Danielle, bundling her coat around her.

He turned to me. "Drive carefully. Call me when you get there."

We kissed—a brief, sad kiss—and I drove off.

Around noon, I turned off the highway onto a country road that ran alongside a river. Danielle and I spread a blanket by the shore and we laid out a picnic of sandwiches and fruit. It was chilly, but we wound our scarves around us. Afterward, while she played alongside the riverbank, I lay back to listen to the soothing sounds of water gliding over the rocks. It was the first time since I had known Yves that I had chosen a spot for a picnic, a quiet off-the-highway place, the kind where I had always wanted to stop but was overruled. It was a small thing, but a comforting one, somehow mitigating the sadness of the moment. Danielle jumped on the blanket and stretched out beside me. She smelled like fresh laundry that had been hung out in the sun to dry. I loved it when she snuggled close to me.

"Is Yves coming soon?" she asked. She called him Yves.

"I don't know, darlingette."

"Why didn't he come with us, Mommy?"

I searched for an answer. Fighting back tears, I looked up at the sky and wondered if this was not merely a temporary separation from the man I had loved so dearly. So much had happened to erode that love. Fear and dread were my emotions now. If I lie on this riverbank long enough, I thought, I could shut everything out of my mind. Except for the soft, repetitive music of the river and an occasional call of a bird, there was silence.

Hours later, we drove into the courtyard at La Salle. The roofs glistened with frost, and an icy wind cut across our faces. The place looked abandoned and grim in the unforgiving glare of late-January light. I pulled up to the house by the road. We owned half of a hamlet but were still banished to the euphemistically christened "temporary" house. Would the work on the main house never be finished? Underscoring the inhospitable welcome, the door was stuck, and it took all my strength to open it. The big, empty room was dismal. Its meter-thick walls had protected the house from the elements, but the air was frigid and damp. We kept our coats tightly wrapped around us while Danielle gathered twigs and I found a few leftover logs around the fireplace. Yves used to say that he was a Sagittarius, a sign of fire, and I was an earth sign; it wasn't in my nature to build fires.

Nevertheless, reaching back to my days as a Girl Scout, I struck a match to the crumpled paper I had stuffed among twigs under the logs, poked, and patiently blew and blew on it until, to my delight, it flickered and the twigs caught on fire. Then quickly and with a crackling sound, the logs ignited and the room became blanketed with a cozy vermilion glow. "Even a Virgo can build a fire!" I proclaimed triumphantly.

"Mitch! Danielle!" Jeanne appeared at the doorway. "I heard your car coming up the hill. I can't believe my eyes! What are you two doing here in the middle of winter? I didn't expect to see you until spring. Come to check up on those lazy workmen? Danielle! Come over here and give your Mémé a kiss. Where's Yves?"

"He—well, he'll come later. Next month, maybe."

"Are you all right, Mitch?" She looked at me and understood.

"I'll be all right now," I said.

We dragged three chairs close to the fireplace.

"Yves always made the fires. But Mommy and I made this one," said Danielle proudly.

"It's blazing away just fine."

We sat for a while, staring at the fire. Jeanne leaned forward in her chair. Her cheeks were flushed, and her eyes mirrored the flicker of the flames. "Marcel will bring over enough firewood to keep this one going. You can't sleep in a freezing house. You both come over for supper tonight."

Danielle tugged at my sleeve. "Can I go and play with Monique?"

"Sure, darlingette. I have to unpack. Just make sure it's all right with Madame Blevenec."

"Come, *ma fille*, your mother has work to do. I'll walk with you to La Sallette. Monique will be glad to see you, *dame*."

She hugged me, took Danielle by the hand, and they went down the hill together. I stayed by the fire, losing myself in the dance of the flames until it seemed I had become one with the sparks scintillating over the logs. Maybe Yves was right. Maybe it was madness to come to La Salle in the middle of winter or to think I could handle La Salle by myself. Yet, I reminded myself, so far I was doing all right. First a picnic along a riverbank. Now, a blazing fire. I leaned back. Then, as if the chimney were swallowing up the bitterness and pain of the past months along with the smoke, the churning I felt inside for so long began to subside. Danielle was at La Sallette playing with Monique. My darling Jeanne had come to greet us. Marcel would bring more logs, and we would have supper with them tonight. A feeling of calm came over me. I felt the tense muscles in my face soften, and with a hesitant sigh of relief, I pulled myself up to unload the car.

14

Clinging Vines

"NATURE TAKES OVER IN A WINK if you aren't on the lookout," Marcel had warned Yves the first spring we came to La Salle. "If you don't keep cutting back those *sacré* briars, before you know it, they'll steal the land and turn it back to wilderness. Took us peasants hundreds of years to tame the land. Can't give it back to the briars now."

Days after returning to La Salle, I was alarmed to see that the thornbushes had flourished while we were away. Fiercely aggressive, they were jutting into paths and encroaching upon precious planting space in the vegetable garden. I went to the garage and reached for Yves' machete. As I pulled it from its rusty hook, the image of his slashing my painting rushed back into my mind. I dusted off the oversize moon-shaped weapon and headed to the vegetable garden. Thick, belligerent stems shot out in all directions like loaded pistols poised for attack. I braced myself. I drew back the machete and swung, and swung again. A few insignificant offshoots drifted to the ground while those remaining retaliated by clawing at my skin. Engrossed in my quarry, I was unaware of blood oozing down my arm.

"Mitch!" Marcel waved frantically from across the road. *"Nom de Dieu!* What in blazes are you doing? Put down that machete!"

I reached for a handkerchief in my pocket and dabbed at the crimson streaks streaming down my arms.

"You trying to kill yourself?" he exclaimed, coming nearer.

"I was just trying to—"

"With a dangerous blade like that? This is no work for you, Mitch. You could have lopped off an arm or a leg. You should have asked me to do it."

"I can't always ask you to do my work, Marcel."

"Mitch," Jeanne shouted, storming across the road. "What the devil are you up to? Put down that *sacré* machete!"

"I was just trying to—"

"Trim those briars? Merde *alors,* you'll kill yourself and everyone else around you."

"That's what I told her, Mémé."

"But Yves used to—"

"You don't know how to cut down thornbushes! You might as well send a baby to stop an army!"

"Okay, okay. Both of you. I'm no expert. But the blade is dull. That's why I can't trim these damned briars."

Jeanne ran her finger along the curve of the blade. "She's right, Marcel. It is dull. You come home with us. I'll take care of your arms while Marcel sharpens it. But if I have my say, Marcel will be doing this from now on. You won't be using this machete again soon!"

In the kitchen, Jeanne went to the cupboard and brought out a glass jar containing cloth for bandages. She boiled water in the iron pot over the fireplace, took down a bunch of dried grasses and herbs hanging over the stove, and dropped it into the water as if she were brewing tea. Several times I had seen her crouch near her vegetable garden, pull up blades of grass, and wrap them in her apron, and had wondered if she had the same instinct as cats and dogs when they scratch through grass to dig for the herbs that cure them. Waiting for the water to cool down, Jeanne wrapped a cloth around my cuts and scratches, and I followed Marcel to the stable where he kept an old whetstone used for sharpening. He skimmed the long, curved blade back and forth across the stone in a dancelike movement that was incongruously graceful and agile for his slow, heavy frame, stopping from time to time to rub his thumb against the blade, shaking his head and saying, *"Encore un peu."* When it was honed to his satisfaction, we returned to the kitchen, where Jeanne was waiting with her concoction.

"I have to do the things Yves used to do," I said, grimacing as pads of cloth infused with the herbs stung the gashes in my arms. "I'll learn to trim those briars—somehow."

"What if your arms had got infected, Mitch?" scolded Marcel. "You'd be laid up and no good to anyone." With his thick, roughened fingers, he was dropping bits of tobacco onto a square of thin paper and meticulously rolling it into a cigarette. Most of the men in the country rolled their own cigarettes. I never saw a woman in the country smoke, although it was said that some did in secret.

"People in the country say 'The only thing worse than a sick wife is a sick cow.' What do they mean, Marcel?"

He ran his tongue along the edge of the paper and folded it over, sealing the dark tobacco inside. "Well, I suppose they mean there's work a woman does on the farm and work a man does, and neither of 'em can do the work of a cow."

"You lucky bastard," exclaimed Jeanne. "I never get sick and our cows are so hardy they could run the farm by themselves."

"But what if the wife does get sick?" I insisted.

Marcel lit the cigarette, took a shallow drag, and blew out the smoke. "It might mean trouble."

"Might!" Jeanne exploded, her gray eyes flashing. "You know as sure as the devil everything falls apart when a woman comes down sick!"

"Now calm down, Mémé," said Marcel, winking at me. "Just wanted to make sure you were paying attention."

"Remember the story about Fotreau?" I said. "Annick managed by herself. And you did too, Jeanne, when you were alone on the farm. So will I."

"I was born on a farm, Mitch. Listen, I remember how you helped out with the hay that first summer you came to La Salle. Be patient. You're strong. In time you'll do most everything. For now, we'll get Eric the day worker to come help you out with the heavy work."

"A day worker? That's admitting I can't do it myself."

"You don't need to prove yourself, *ma fille*. Even the toughest peasant hires day workers to help out. Eric will trim the bushes and chop your wood."

"Well . . ."

"You can hire Eric when you need him."

"I guess I could use the help. How much do I pay him?"

"Give him all the cider he can drink, three meals, and snacks. He'll be happy with that."

"But how much do I pay him?"

"Nobody pays the day workers, Mitch," said Marcel.

Two days later, thin and wiry, with his clothes dangling over a bony frame, Eric the day worker appeared at our door. He was sun-scorched, with translucent skin barely covering a prominent nose, and several obstinately remaining teeth gleamed in the sunlight when he opened his mouth to speak. I didn't understand a word he said. Not yet sober from the day before, he followed me unevenly first to the pile of logs to be chopped, then to the vegetable garden along the road where the thornbushes were urgently in need of trimming. I handed him the ax and machete and bolted over to Jeanne's house as if chased by a wild boar.

"He's drunk!" I cried, catching my breath.

Jeanne continued stirring something in a heavy pot over the iron grill.

"Jeanne, did you hear me? He's drunk from yesterday. If I give him one more ounce of cider, it will be homicide!"

"Poor soul's been drunk since the day he was born, Mitch. Never saw him sober. Don't you mind about him. He sleeps in an empty barn, helps folks out when they need him, and gets fed. That's all he wants. He'll think you're cheating him if he doesn't get his fill of cider."

Eric gulped down all the cider I offered. He gobbled breakfast, lunch, supper, and intermittent snacks with the frenzied intensity of a squirrel storing up for winter. He worked through the long day, sliced off branches as thick as my ankles as if they were twigs, and chopped enough wood to last for two weeks. At the end of the day, I impulsively handed him a bill of a thousand francs. How could I hire someone without paying anything? He stared at the bill in disbelief. Then he broke into a broad, nearly toothless smile, and a scaly hand shot out to grab it. "*Merci, merci,* Ma'am Drumont. Any time you want Eric to come round, you just say so."

Two dollars was a ridiculous amount of money for all the work he had done and seemed like exploitation. Yet Marcel had said not to pay him at all. Why wasn't Yves here? He understood the customs in the French countryside that were still such a mystery to me. He knew how to talk to the peasants. Sometimes I was completely bewildered by what was happening to me. What was a Chicago girl doing on an isolated farm, alone with a young child, in the middle of nowhere? Admittedly, it was my idea to come here alone, but now that I was here, how could I manage without him? The worst part was that I missed him. Not the Yves of late, of course, who had changed, who had given unreasonable orders, who had frightened and hurt me, but the man with whom I had fallen in love and whom I couldn't put out of my mind, no matter how hard I tried.

15

Sticks and Stones

"Loïc from Questembert, of all God's children! What brings you to La Salle?" Jeanne called to a man waving at her from across the road. Short, solid, and muscular, he looked as if he had been carved out of stone.

"Working for the Calaix brothers in Vannes now, Mémé," he called back. "Come to work on the old Blevenec house."

"You better watch him, Mitch," Jeanne said, shaking her fist at him as he crossed the road. "He's an old scoundrel from way back."

"I wouldn't dare screw up now that I got you staring over my shoulder, Mémé," he replied.

"Jeanne, I think you know everyone in the Morbihan," I said.

"Everyone knows Mémé," said Loïc, kissing her twice on both cheeks.

"Come in for a glass of cider, both of you. You've got the best stonemason in the business, Mitch," she said, patting him on the back. "You're in good hands now."

As the Calaix brothers had promised, we now had plumbers, carpenters, and masons who appreciated the old stone buildings. Floors had to be laid, walls created, roofs repaired, doors and windows invented, all the while preserving the tradition and integrity of the old Breton farmhouse. The main house would be a combination living room and kitchen. Twenty feet away, the cluster of buildings that had been the stable, pigsty, and dairy would be our bedrooms. As long as the weather was mild, the separation between the two was not a problem, but in the winter months, when it was cold, windy, and raining, we would be deluged every time we had to get from one part of the house to another.

One morning, I overheard Roger talking about the ruins of an old abandoned château on a hillside on the road to Redon.

"You mean ruins with old stones?" I asked.

"*Dame*, yes. The hillside is covered with them."

"Do you think people can cart them away?"

"They've been sitting like ducks waiting to be shot for twenty, thirty years. Can't see why not."

I drew a sketch of the two living areas and the gap between. "What do you think, Roger? Would there be enough stones to build a corridor between the two?"

"As many corridors as you want. I'll ask Fernand of Kerlomen to take us there with his tractor."

An hour later, Roger, Marcel, Jeanne, and I piled on the back of Fernand's tractor. Chugging up the hill to the remains of the château, we saw stones everywhere. Some were buried and hardly visible, some peeked through dirt or rubble, and others were in full sight. Propped up in the middle as if welcoming us with open arms were the magnificent sculpted mantelpieces of two fireplaces; nearby were stones that fit along the sides. We dragged them to a clearing in the rubble and pieced them together like children playing with a giant three-dimensional jigsaw puzzle. Jeanne was a born excavator. Notwithstanding her age, she climbed nimbly to the top of each pile. With her long black skirt swirling in the wind, she stood like a mythic priestess on a mountaintop, reaching out with both arms and calling, "Come, all of you. Look what I found!" Later that morning, I saw her lifting a large stone and went to help. "Look, Mitch," she said. "This one's rounded, like a part of a circle." After digging and scratching, we unearthed two more stones that fit together with it to form an arch.

I hugged her. "You're an angel! These stones will be the archway for our new front door!"

For the rest of the day, we foraged through the rubble. Each time the tractor was full, we rode back to La Salle to empty our bounty into the courtyard. As soon as the workers from the Calaix brothers helped slide the precious cargo off the tractor, we climbed back for another trip. By dusk, we had collected more than enough stones for a passageway to connect the buildings. Loïc and I decided the addition would become the entrance with a front door opening onto the courtyard and a back door to the woods behind the houses. We found stones for two fireplaces, stones for replacing the ugly slabs of cement around doors and windows, and enough stones to give the entire façade an all-over face-lift.

Forsythia shrubs were beginning to bloom, a sign of early spring, and the work on the main house that had slowed to a stop over winter months picked up again. Workmen were laying large square rust-colored tiles with precision

and care. Masons were roughly plastering walls in prepara-
tion for a final, smooth finish. I preferred the unfinished,
rustic look and told them to leave it that way. Carpenters
were scraping, cleaning, and polishing wooden rafters encrusted with centuries of smoke and dirt, and painters were
plastering and painting white the smoke-blackened spaces
between them. Through windows carved out of meter-thick
walls on either side of the fireplace and through a bay window over the kitchen sink, sunlight poured into the once-
somber house.

I was installing comforts I had always taken for granted.
To me, they were basic necessities of life, but in the farms
and hamlets of the Morbihan as well as in most parts of the
globe, they were unknown. Central heating, a bathroom
with a tub and shower, an indoor toilet, an aluminum kitchen
sink with hot and cold running water, all these underscored
the cavernous gap between the way I had grown up and the
way of life of my current neighbors. Jeanne had spent her
life chopping wood and building fires for heat. Until recent
years, she had had neither running water nor electricity in the
house, and many farms in the region were still without. Her
outhouse was yards away from the house. Yet, she admired
everything I was installing in the house without the slightest
hint of envy. "Mitch, *que c'est beau!*" she said, running her
hand over the blue and white ceramic counterspace in the
kitchen, and when I showed her my refrigerator with an
oversize freezer compartment on top, she exclaimed, "Why,
it's big enough to freeze half a pig and vegetables and have
them all year round!" Whenever she killed one of her animals, she cured or smoked the meat to keep it from spoiling,
and toward the end of summer, when most of the fruits and

vegetables ripened at once, she put up preserves and jams so they would last throughout the winter. Nevertheless, much of the harvest went to waste. Recently I had bought her a gas water heater for her kitchen so she wouldn't have to heat water in a heavy iron kettle over coals in the fireplace. As soon as I could, I would buy her a freezer. An enormous one where she could freeze an entire pig if she wanted to.

As the houses began to take shape, Jeanne helped me decide where to put a cupboard, where tables and benches should go, and how many wooden chests I would need. Thanks to Jean Bonbon, the mobile grocer, or from chatting with people from other villages at Mass on Sunday, she always knew when one of the peasants in the region was having a farm sale. She came with me to the auctions where, along with selling off farm equipment, peasants were eager to rid themselves of old wooden tables, carved cabinets, and wooden chests and replace them with modern furniture of plastic and Formica.

"I'll never understand how they can part with these beautiful things," I said to her at one of the auctions. "They're irreplaceable; antique shops in Paris sell them for a fortune!"

"Not so loud," she said in a stage whisper, poking me with her elbow. "They'll up their prices."

For my kitchen, we picked out a long wooden table with deep nicks and scratches that had served in a convent for centuries. For next to nothing, we found wooden benches, a whimsically carved cupboard of luminous blond oak for dishes and towels, and three ample, sturdy wooden chests that would contain everything we owned. Decorated with carved initials and roughly chiseled flourishes, they had been built hundreds of years ago as dowry chests for storing the linens and dreams of brides as they ventured into uncertain futures.

Square foot by square foot, with Jeanne's and Marcel's help, we cleaned up the courtyard. Loading cartons and wheelbarrows over and over with debris that had accumulated over decades, we made countless trips to empty them into a ditch the workmen had dug deep in the woods beyond where Yves had built his studio. I ordered truckloads of new gravel for the courtyard and soil for planting flowers around the new entrance. Rerouting a fragrant old wisteria plant that climbed the wall of the main house, Jeanne and I coaxed it to arch gracefully over our front door, now framed with the stones she had discovered among the ruins of the château. Behind the main house, where Madame Blevenec had tended her flower garden, I planted my favorite flowers, dahlias and peonies, to commingle with her lilac and rosebushes. To extend the living area into the outdoors, Loïc helped me build a stone patio for a table, chairs, and a California-style barbecue. Three apple trees grew at the far end of the garden near the woods. Not wanting to offend the villagers who covered themselves from head to foot even in the heat of summer, I wore a knee-length man's shirt over my bikini. But the apple trees camouflaged a secluded spot where I could sunbathe naked and abandon myself to the warm breezes. In the earliest morning hours, before the sun could be glimpsed through the mist, I practiced yoga and sat in a lotus position at the edge of the garden under an old peach tree, its gnarled branches reaching out to sea like an old dancer suspended in a final triumphant arabesque.

At last, the main house and bedrooms were finished. Although saddened that Yves was not with us to share the long-awaited transfer, Danielle and I readied ourselves to make the bittersweet move into our new quarters. We emptied our clothes, bedcovers, pots, and pans onto a wheelbarrow and giddily wheeled our way across the courtyard to the house we had waited for, for so long.

⌒

Two weeks after we moved into the main house, Yves came to visit. How painful it must have been for him to revisit the hamlet he had discovered and loved from the start. Danielle ran to him, hugged and kissed him. She led him first to her room and then showed him the rest of the houses. She held on tightly to his hand and didn't let go. She had missed him so much, and against all reason, so had I. Time and distance dimmed bitter memories, and into the void crept wistful illusions, beguiling me to brush logic aside. "Love doesn't disappear without a trace," an inner voice cajoled me. "Danielle needs her father. You were so right for each other. After all, it was his illness—his 'cyclic personality,' as the doctor had said—that made him act the way he did. He seems calm now. Maybe he's seeing a doctor. Taking medication. If only he were taking medication! At least give it a chance. Maybe the clock will turn back, and everything will be as it was in the beginning . . ."

After the dinner Danielle and I had prepared and fussed over, she climbed on his lap. It seemed so natural to see him sitting at the head of the table. "Will you stay with us now?" Danielle asked him eagerly.

He smiled and kissed her on the forehead.

We crossed the road to Jeanne's house for coffee and cake. The air was festive.

"You know the big bay window Mitch insisted on putting in the bathroom, Yves," said Marcel. "She made it big enough for the whole village to enjoy the sights."

"No one ever uses that path," I protested, blushing.

"They will now, *dame*," said Marcel.

"*Mon vieux*, if I catch you on that path, your hide will spice up my next *pot au feu*!" said Jeanne.

We laughed, and so did Yves.

"Mitch did a lot of work on those houses while you were away," said Marcel.

"She was always good at that," Yves said.

"She's been showing folks around here how to fix up these old farmhouses to look like new. Old man Dorso and his bulldozer will have to look for another line of work, if she has her way." Marcel refilled our glasses with cider. "You here to stay, Yves?"

"Not yet," he replied. "I've got too much to do in Paris." He turned to me. "Besides, it's your house now. That's what you always wanted, isn't it?"

A chill spread over the room. What made him say that? He was the one who had discovered La Salle. Only later, when I learned to love it too, did it become ours. Our exchanges were strained, in stark contrast to Jeanne and Marcel's. Warmth and humor infused everything they said to each other. When they teased each other, it underscored their mutual affection. They knew each other's thoughts before they spoke. Yves and I had had that once. We couldn't wait to be alone together and had a language of our own that only we could understand. In spite of myself, in spite of all that had happened, the memory of those feelings persisted.

We returned home and put Danielle to bed. The moon

was full and lit up the night sky as if luring us to delight in its luminescence. "Let's take a walk in the woods," he said, taking my arm. How many times had I walked alone in the woods, wondering if he would ever again be at my side. My heart leaped at the thought of it, and we set off silently, arm in arm into the woods.

After a while, Yves said, "It's good coming back. I've missed La Salle. I've missed Danielle." After a pause he added, "I missed you, too."

The night was mild. How fragrant was the sweet smell of the pine trees.

"You were right about Jeanne. You and she are really close. I can see that."

"She calls me the daughter she never had. I'm so lucky to have her nearby."

The play of moonlight and shadows through the trees beckoned us to walk deeper into the woods.

"Why did you look so surprised when I said La Salle was your house?" he said.

"Did I look surprised?"

"Of course you did. Everybody noticed."

"It was never my house. It was ours."

"Why do you contradict me?"

"I'm not. I'm just saying—"

"There you go. Just like always. You're a petite bourgeoise who has to have her own way. You'll never change."

His voice became agitated. He grabbed my arm. A feeling of terror shot through me. I must be crazy. What am I doing in the woods? With no one in earshot. Alone with a man who could become dangerous any second! In a steadied voice, I said, "I'm going back now, Yves. It's late. I'm tired."

His eyes flashed. He spun me around. "We'll go back when I say we will. It's time you learn to do as I tell you."

"Okay. But please, I don't like leaving Danielle alone after dark."

We turned back without speaking.

Yves insisted on sleeping in my bed that night, although we never touched. I laid awake for hours, painfully mindful of the empty darkness that separated us. When I finally fell asleep, I dreamed he appeared to me across an abyss. I called to him, but I had no voice. Floodwaters raged around us, hurling our bodies together and ripping them apart, all the while in eerie silence. I screamed, but there was no sound. When I awoke, startled, I lay motionless while thoughts raced across my mind, wounding me over and over again, longing for the tenderness and love we had once felt for each other, knowing they were gone forever.

He kissed Danielle goodbye and left the next morning.

⌒

Painted in thick impasto, Yves' searing portrait of an owl that was part bird and part bark of the tree he was perched in seemed to observe with burning eyes the world around him from the kitchen wall. Across the room, a dark and unsettling crow fixed his stare over the table where we ate. A melancholic painting of a lone figure leaning against a massive tree trunk hung on my bedroom wall. From the beginning, I had loved Yves' paintings and had wanted to be surrounded by them. But the day he left, I removed them all. In place of the lone figure in my bedroom, I hung one of my oil landscapes painted in cerulean blues, olive greens, and yellows shimmering over hills and grassy meadows. Two airy and sunlit seascapes dispossessed the owl and the crow. After pounding hooks into the walls and adjusting the paintings, I stood back and saw that the atmosphere in the house had been completely recast. In a single gesture, I had disentangled myself from his vision and reclaimed my own. Without knowing it, by removing his paintings, I had sealed the end of my marriage.

⁓

For the first time in years, I was painting every day. Waking each morning at dawn along with the peasants, I hastened to begin before the brashness of the sun delineated harsh lights and shadows, carving out sharp outlines of trees, hills, and horizon. In summer, the heat was so intense it was a streak of fire on my back and soaked up the moisture on the paper, making it difficult to work with the transparency and fluidity of watercolor. But on cool days, or on days when the fog lingered and moisture hung in the air, I could blend the light of the morning mist with the emerging sun, lay color over color like a theme in a fugue that fades as another unfolds, softly at first, then gradually asserts itself to the foreground, retreating and repeating itself, but each time in a different way, making complex, haunting music. Painting had always given me indescribable pleasure. And painful as it had been to paint in secret, it remained my hidden joy. But ever since I had left Yves in Paris and returned to La Salle, and especially since I had removed his paintings from the walls and replaced them with my own, all my fears and constraints of the past had vanished. No one in the world would ever again tell me what I could or could not paint. Never again would I paint furtively, or paint a small canvas so it might be easy to hide, or pray that the paint would dry so I could stash it behind the chicken coop or under a wheelbarrow, fearful of being discovered, fearful of everything. Like an animal escaped from a cage, I had broken loose. I was free to be myself. Wild and free, I would paint as big as I wanted and leave the canvases in the open, uncovered, for all the world to see. In the afternoons I splashed oil paints on large canvases. In the mornings, I worked with my beloved watercolors, feeling I was a part of the sunrise—part of the universe, at one with nature. I was euphoric. At times like these, I could paint forever.

"You sure have a knack of putting down on paper what you see in front of you, Mitch," Jeanne said when I showed her an emerald and burnt ocher seascape I had done that morning at the gulf at low tide.

"Would you like to have it?"

"*Dame, oui.* I'll hang it right here over the kitchen table. How much can I pay you for it?"

"We'll make a deal. I'll get it framed in Vannes, and if it's all right with you, I'll exchange it for a sack of potatoes."

"Two sacks of potatoes and a basket of shallots." She tapped the table with her fist. We shook hands and hugged to seal the transaction.

Seeing my paintings in other people's houses had always given me a thrill. But nothing compared with the joy of seeing my seascape over the scarred wooden table in Jeanne's kitchen and next to the frayed amber-tinted wedding picture of her and Luc Diquero.

16

Night Callers

IT WAS A QUIET SPRING EVENING, marked only by the occasional stir of a breeze grazing across the courtyard like a muted sigh. Danielle and I were busily engaged, drawing a picture and making up a story to go with it, when we heard a commotion outside. I peered out the front door. To my surprise, Eric the day worker was weaving and stumbling in the entranceway. He flashed his usual grin of a carved-out pumpkin with a flickering candle inside and mumbled something that I didn't understand.

"Eric. What are you doing here at this hour? Do you know what time it is?"

"Sure do, M'am Drummah. S'late." Slurring his words more than usual, he was very drunk.

"Yes, it is. Now go home. I'll let you know when I need you."

"Beh, me an' my pals, we come t'pay yuh a visit."

"Pals?"

Abruptly he spun around and shouted hoarsely to several

blurred shapes that were barely visible in the shadows. Like phantoms eerily coming into focus, two figures emerged in the night light, waved their arms, zigzagged across the court-yard with a drunken gait, and staggered in the direction of the house.

"Who are you? Go home—all of you. *Now!*" I backed inside the house and slammed the door. Danielle stood close beside me.

"Don't worry, honey," I said, inhaling and exhaling slowly and trying to remain calm. Escalating shouting, stomping, hooting, and pounding on the door brought to mind scenes from Old West movies, of bloodthirsty Indians surrounding the house of a desperate pioneer woman who has barricaded herself and her child in the house in a brave attempt to keep the savages from breaking down the door—for what purpose I didn't dare remember. Cursing myself for not having put hefty locks and bolts on windows and doors that would have kept these drunken intruders out, I pressed my body weight against the door. To my horror, it burst open and three inebriated scarecrows stumbled inside.

"Get out of here this instant," I commanded in a voice as authoritative as I could muster. They shot past me as if I didn't exist and lunged into the kitchen. I glanced at Da-nielle to reassure her, and saw that she was alarmed too.

"Hey, Gaston! Cedrick! *Venez ici.* Come over 'n' pay respects to the ladies," roared Eric, swaying and garbling his words. The three men whispered hoarsely among themselves and started toward us, falling over themselves, rolling their heads and waving their arms as if performing some kind of nightmarish dance.

I stopped breathing. I swung around, searching for a

nonexistent shotgun, baseball bat, anything with which to protect my baby, my hearth, and my home. Nothing was in sight. I had only my fists. Bare fists to overpower a gang of three drunken hoodlums. Oh, God. Suddenly there was a crashing sound in the entranceway. In unison, Danielle, the three uninvited guests, and I spun 180 degrees to face the door. Everyone watched as if hypnotized when, like a vision, Jeanne Montrelay appeared silhouetted in the doorway, brandishing a pitchfork.

"*Merde!*" she yelled at the top of her voice. The word reverberated throughout the room. "You goddamn fool bastards! Eric! Cedrick! Gaston! What the devil are you doing at La Salle this time of night?"

"Wuh-wait a minute, Mé-Mémé," Eric stammered, diving behind a chair. "D-d-don't be mad. Just wanted my pals to meet the ch-ch-chatelaine of La-la-la Salle."

"You drunken sonofabitch. Get your goddamn tail out of here and take your guzzling buddies with you!" She charged inside with the gleaming prongs of her pitchfork aimed at the three of them as they cowered behind a chair and the table, trembling and eyeing her as if Lucifer himself had risen from middle earth.

". . . and if I ever see any of you coming back here all liquored up like this, I swear I'll impale every last one of you! By God, I'll start right now." She lunged toward them, shrieking what sounded like a stream of curses in Gallo.

Like frightened monkeys, they scampered over and under the table, stumbled past Danielle and me, catapulted out the door, and half crawling, half running, disappeared into the night. Jeanne slammed the door behind her and marched back inside. We stood for a moment, frozen, staring at each other. Then we started to laugh. We couldn't stop laughing until we cried.

"Oh, Jeanne darling," I said. "I was so scared. I've never been so glad to see anyone in my whole life!"

"I saw them stagger into your courtyard. Would have gotten here sooner but I had to get this pitchfork from the stable." She brandished it for emphasis, launching another round of laughter. "They just wanted to see the chatelaine."

"The *what*?"

"That's what folks around here call you, Mitch. 'The Chatelaine of La Salle.'"

"What's a 'chatelaine,' Mommy?"

"It's a lady of the manor, darlingette," I said, wiping tears from my eyes. "That's the funniest thing I ever heard. But I can't let Eric come back to work for me."

"Sure you can, Mitch. He won't soon forget what happened tonight. You don't need to worry about him or his pals."

"I wasn't afraid," said Danielle wisely. "Eric's nice."

"You're right, *ma petite*," said Jeanne. "They're all nice and harmless enough. But they shouldn't drink and go carousing. They won't be back, though. That's for sure."

Danielle climbed on Jeanne's lap, and we sat around the table, laughing and telling stories until it was way past time to put her to bed.

⌒

"I hear you had visitors last night," said Thérèse the next afternoon. "I brought you an extra pup we didn't want to put to sleep. He'll grow up to be a watchdog for you. You need protection, Mitch." She was cradling in the palm of her hand a furry white puppy with black spots, the least threatening creature I had ever seen.

"We'd love to have a dog, wouldn't we, Danielle?"

"What's his name?"

"He's too little," said Thérèse. "He hasn't had time for a name yet."

"Will he scare away the bad people?"

"He'll bark at strangers," said Thérèse.

We turned to the puppy. Accommodatingly, he barked as loud as he could for his size. We named him Pierrot and immediately integrated him into our household.

"How can I thank you, Thérèse?"

"You don't owe me anything, Mitch. You and Danielle shouldn't be alone on the farm." We kissed on both cheeks, and she went back across the road.

17

A Helping Hand

IT WAS RARE THAT A CAR drove into the courtyard, but when one did, Pierrot tried his best to fulfill his role as a watchdog. The morning three grim, portly ladies arrived at La Salle, he bristled, charged outside, barked ferociously for two seconds, and then welcomed them with all his heart. I had never seen them before and went out to greet them too.

"A pleasure, Madame Drumont," one of them said, getting out of the car and thrusting forward a gloved hand to shake mine.

"We trust we're not disturbing you, *chère madame*," chirped the second in a saccharine-sweet voice.

The third and most imposing of the three introduced herself as Madame Loèst. "We have come to discuss an important matter with you," she announced as one accustomed to being in control.

What in the world could these overdressed, gloved, and hatted creatures be doing at La Salle? The thought occurred to me that they might be a welcoming committee. But from where? I was hardly new to the region. Maybe they were from a charitable organization. Did they want me to contribute to their good works? At a loss as to what to say to them, I offered tea.

"Excellent idea," said Madame Loèst and started marching toward the house.

"But first," I said, blocking her path, "I'd like to know the reason for the visit."

"The child is in school?" asked one of them, stealing a glance around and lowering her voice.

"She is."

"The school in Sulniac with the gypsy children, *n'est-ce pas?*" said the one with a sugary voice. She smiled, uncovering small, pointed crocodile teeth.

"My daughter goes to a very good school in Sulniac," I replied firmly, having changed my mind about tea.

"*Chère madame,*" said Madame Loèst. "Permit me to get to the point. You can be certain we have come here with only your best interests at heart—yours, and of course, the little one's. Let me explain. We are members of a committee from the Saint Therèsa and Saint Anthony Church in Vannes." A beatific smile failed to lift her sagging jowls. "Our committee is dedicated to helping families in need."

"In need of what?" I asked, becoming increasingly defensive.

"Madame Drumont," said the next in line. "It has been proven many times over that children at the tender age of your daughter—she is five, *n'est-ce pas?*—must be raised by both parents in order to enjoy a healthy childhood. Otherwise, results may be tragic. *Tragique!*"

"That is no exaggeration," interjected the one with

pointed teeth. "We are not suggesting you are not doing your best, *ma pauvre* Madame Drumont. *Mon Dieu!* Heaven forbid. But it is well documented that a woman alone in this world is at a great disadvantage in the raising of a child."

"What are you suggesting?"

"Alors," said Madame Loèst brightly, energized by the way the meeting was proceeding. "We are prepared to place your child in a loving, churchgoing family where she will have the benefit of both mother and father. Perhaps you haven't considered this until now, Madame Drumont, but we assure you we are here to help. It is never too late to save a child's future and, more important, we must add, her soul."

I tried to steady my voice. "What you are suggesting is out of the question. Neither my daughter's future nor her soul need your help now—or ever!"

"But Madame Dru—" one of them began.

"You understand, Madame Drumont, we are only here for the good of the little one," another of them called after me as I went inside and slammed the door. My God. Who could have let loose these three Lady Macbeths? Yves never would have done that. Nor would anyone in the village. I swore that if I ever found out who was responsible, I would strangle them. How dare they come here and suggest such a thing? Take Danielle away from me? As easily as if they were dragging a calf from a cow? I tried to think of something to take my mind off them. Wash dishes. Mop the floor. Hang the laundry. But their faces kept coming back. What's worse, doubts kept creeping in. Could there be a grain of truth to what they were saying? Of course the separation had been hard on Danielle. Of course she missed her father terribly. And it was true I could never be both mother and father to her. But if I was a good mother, if she felt secure, and if she was a happy and healthy child, wasn't that enough? Was there a chance they could come back and steal my child away from me? I shuddered and tried to erase the three witches from my mind. It was impossible; they were fragments of a nightmare one never forgets.

Silent and remote, protected by miles and miles of woods like so many isolated hamlets and villages around the globe, La Salle was a world contained unto itself. Often I wondered how many women lived alone on their farms, for whatever reason, and how they managed to endure the loneliness. Sometimes the seclusion was a comfort, a solace, but it was also a stifling weight pressing down on me. After Yves' visit, I could no longer delude myself into believing we might one day get back together. But living on an isolated farm in the rural countryside of France, what chance was there in that vast, distant universe out there of meeting someone else? Someone I might care for and who could be a loving father to Danielle? Of course, there was the lecherous white-haired real estate agent from Vannes with the body shape of a crab. He drove by La Salle from time to time, and sometimes I spotted him leering at me through the forsythia bushes be-yond the vegetable garden as I planted seeds and pulled weeds and even once from the bushes surrounding the apple trees as I was stretched out blissfully naked in the sun. And there was the married, illiterate electrician who abruptly thrust a bony, hairy hand on my knee as we drove in his tiny car to get supplies in Theix.

Still, I had grown accustomed to living in the country. I had come to know and love the villagers. Danielle was everything I could wish for in a child, and Jeanne had become a central part of my life. In the afternoons, though, when all the villagers were in the fields and Danielle was at school, it would strike me how alone I was. I could hear no muted sounds of voices. No shadow of a stranger could be seen passing by. Even if I shouted as loud as I could, no one was there to hear me. I was utterly alone. At moments like this, loneliness swept over me like waves rising and falling on a beach. Sometimes, when those feelings overwhelmed me, I would take long walks through my pine forest, brush my fingers over the bark of the trees, and lean against a tree for strength.

One tree in particular comforted me. I knew by heart the path through the forest to find it. It was an exceptionally graceful pine tree, with a sturdy trunk and sinewy branches that reached around and seemed to draw me close to it. I would stretch my arms around the trunk, press my body against its bark, and feel the life force of the tree throb and flow into me, as if I were having intimate contact with another living being. The thought made me smile; had I become physically attracted to a tree? I sank down on a nearby tree trunk and began to laugh. All by myself in the woods, I laughed. How absurd life was. I couldn't remember the last time I had made love. Had this tree come along to sustain me until something, someone, a more appropriate suitor came into my life? Someone like the Yves I once knew? Someone who would never hurt me, who would put his arms around me and protect me like the branches of my pine tree. I had grown up in a big city. I always had family and friends around me. I had never known loneliness before. But I was learning to live with it now as a part of life, a constant ache, a dim yearning I carried with me wherever I went, as I struggled with weeds or planted a new crop of potatoes, the same shrouded, unspoken feeling with no name that Jeanne must have felt while Luc was a prisoner of war, and again after he died, the same feeling so many women have endured in secluded farmhouses around the world since the beginning of time.

18

Nowhere to Hide

"Nom de Dieu!" muttered Marcel, shaking his head and plunging his shovel into the soil. "Will people never learn to stop killing each other?"

"What's going on, Marcel?" I leaned over the fence.

"Heard about it on the radio this morning, Mitch. There's a war going on in the Middle East."

"There is? Who's fighting?"

"The Arabs and Israel."

I had no idea there was even a risk of war. I've become a hermit, I said to myself.

It was June 1967. I drove to Vannes, bought a radio, returned home, and turned on the news. A deep and reverent announcer's voice resonated throughout the kitchen:

> *Le petit état d'Israël*, a people the world considered farmers and nonfighters, in six brief and bewildering days has overcome incalculable odds and has devastated the enemies that surrounded

her. *Mesdames et messieurs*, the Six-Day War in
the Middle East—is over!

The Six-Day War brought home to me how insulated my
life had become. Perhaps as a reaction to the breakup with
Yves, little by little I had enclosed myself in a cocoon as if
the rest of the world didn't exist. While the revelation came
as a shock, still, there was a positive side. La Salle was a safe
haven, a hideaway far removed from whatever danger might
erupt outside.

One thing was certain: no matter how crazed and violent
the world became, we would not go hungry. Sprouting up all
around us was nature's bounty. The first time I dug into the
ground with a shovel and lifted a mound of dirt spilling over
with those golden nuggets commonly known as potatoes, I
thought I had uncovered a miracle. "The earth is teeming
with them," I shouted to an empty village, "and they are
free!" Growing my own vegetables, digging in the soil, and
feeling dirt embedded in my palms and under my fingernails
were new and rapturous sensations, making me feel closer to
the earth than I ever imagined possible back in Chicago. My
garden, on the other hand, had a mind of its own. Madame
Blevenec had maintained her garden with impeccable rows of
every legume imaginable. The day she moved down the hill,
armies of weeds invaded the place, and since the garden ran
alongside the road in full view of neighbors and passersby, it
was a nagging source of embarrassment.

The summer months slipped by, and although I didn't
fully understand why, my incipient gardening efforts began
to show results. Delicate shoots and stems emerged without
my intervention, prompting me to ask, "What could that

be?" or, "Did I plant that?" Soon I could point to an impressive array of vegetables swaying in unison in an increasingly weed-free environment. Somewhat perplexed, I added gardening to my list of recently acquired accomplishments.

One day, I stopped across the road to tell Jeanne that Danielle and I were going to the Gulf of Morbihan for a few days and to ask her to look after Pierrot. We checked into the inn where Yves, Danielle, and I had stayed that first spring. I swam in the bay among the boats. Danielle and I walked in the woods and had supper on the terrace of the auberge overlooking the tiny harbor, just as we had done four years earlier with Yves. Strangely, I felt no sadness because of his absence. In fact, it was liberating to be there on my own. The next morning, however, as I set out my tubes of watercolors and arranged my brushes on the same rickety pier where we had painted sunsets together, I was struck by pangs of nostalgia. I brushed them quickly aside and began to paint. Then, as frequently happens in Brittany, without warning the sky darkened and the weather worsened. A gust of wind ripped my paper from the pier and sent it sailing like a gossamer kite over the water. My creative urges were inundated by an unannounced downpour. The thought crossed my mind that Yves was showing his disapproval of my returning to the inn without him.

The storm struck only along the gulf. As Danielle and I headed inland, clouds dissolved like evanescent puffs of smoke to uncover sunlit ultramarine skies. Driving up the hill to La Salle, we saw a familiar figure dressed in black, bent over in our vegetable garden.

"Jeanne," I called out. "What are you doing?" I parked the car by the garden.

"Mitch! Danielle! What in the name of God are you doing back so soon?" Propping herself up with a shovel, she rose to her feet. "You're supposed to be at the gulf," she said, folding her arms across her chest. "You weren't coming back 'til day after tomorrow!"

"Our plans changed. Now, *ma chèrie* Jeanne, what are you doing in our garden?"

Danielle climbed on the fence alongside of me.

Jeanne hesitated for a minute and tilted her face as she often did like a bird cocking its head. "The truth is, Mitch, I was passing by this morning, and . . ."

"Passing by, indeed! How can I have been so dense!" I rolled my eyes skyward. "That's why millions of weeds disappeared like magic. That's why all those little green things are sprouting up over there. I don't remember planting them. I don't even know what they are! It's you, you trespasser. You've been digging up weeds and planting things in our garden every time I turned my back. All the while I thought I had become a prize gardener!"

Jeanne came to the fence and put a hand on my shoulder. "You will. You will, Mitch. Just not overnight."

"Are you angry with Jeanne, Mommy?" asked Danielle.

"No, darlingette, far from it." I turned to Jeanne. "So, all along, whenever I drove off, whenever I went to the market in Vannes or to paint at the gulf, you've been sneaking over here to undo my mistakes. Good Lord. We would have starved without you. Come inside for a glass of cider, and I won't call the gendarmes—this time."

It was a late August afternoon, the kind of hot summer day when the air trembles like a soprano's vibrato and everything is still as if waiting for the high note to end, when Pierrot's barking ripped through the sultry silence. "Quiet, Pierrot!" I reprimanded mechanically. As Pierrot had grown in size, so had his conviction that he was the legitimate guardian of our household. But he loved everyone indiscriminately, and after an initial display of force, he would leap up to welcome the visitor and then flop over in a spread-eagle position to be petted.

"A fine watchdog!" I said.

"He is a good watchdog," said Danielle, defending him. "He barks."

He kept on barking. It wasn't his usual exuberant greeting for people he knew, nor his token growl for strangers. His high-pitched yapping sounded misplaced and urgent. I went outside to see what was bothering him, and as I stepped into the courtyard, something silvery gray and mud-colored swept past me and slithered into the house.

"Merde." I gasped. "A viper!"

Jeanne had warned us about vipers. They didn't intentionally bite, but they could be deadly if they thought they were being attacked. And now, one was in the house. But where? Where did it go? Almost certainly it headed toward the bedrooms. I slammed the door to the bedrooms, grabbed Danielle by the hand, and ran outside. The only thing I could think of was finding Jeanne and Marcel. As we ran into the courtyard, I saw Jeanne marching across the road. She was clutching her weapon of choice, the pitchfork.

"I heard Pierrot barking," she yelled.

"A viper got in the house!" I shouted back.

"*Nom de Dieu!* Where is he?"

166

"I don't know. In the bedrooms, I think. I'm not sure. Oh, Jeanne, he could be anywhere."

"You stay by the door with Danielle and Pierrot to let me know if he slips outside," she said and stormed into the house like a general forging ahead of her troops while we underlings, meek and anxious, stood behind guarding the entrance. We waited, motionless, our eyes fixed on the ground where the enemy might at any moment attempt an escape. Pierrot remained at our sides, whimpering, his spotted, furry body trembling like a small bird. The courtyard was quiet as if it were holding its breath. We waited. And waited. Suddenly the hot and humid silence was ruptured by an outburst of yelling and swearing in Gallo, French, Breton, and patois. We heard the dragging of furniture, crashing and banging noises from inside the house, and then silence. A minute later the door swung open and Jeanne swept into the courtyard, flourishing the viper writhing and twisting from one of the curved prongs of her pitchfork like an undulating belly dance to a strain of exotic music.

"This bastard won't be scaring anyone from now on," she proclaimed victoriously.

Pierrot began barking wildly again, circling Jeanne and the snake, leaping up and down while maintaining a prudent distance. Danielle began to cry. She tugged at Jeanne's apron. "You're not going to kill him, are you?"

"Of course not, *petite*," she lied, glancing sideways at me. "Now you and Pierrot go back inside the house." As we walked to the road, she whispered, "He was under her bed, Mitch. Thank God Pierrot warned us. He saved her life."

"You both did, Jeanne," I said and kissed her twice on both cheeks as the viper, dangling over our heads, squirmed helplessly in a vain attempt to avoid his fate. She continued across the road, and I turned back to the house to reassure Danielle and give our beloved Pierrot a well-deserved treat.

⌒

Often on crisp, fall evenings, Danielle and I went to Jeanne and Marcel's house for supper, or they came across the road to be with us. When Marcel stayed for supper at Thérèse and Roger's house, I could hear Jeanne's slow and steady footsteps crackling across the gravel in the courtyard. She would arrive at our doorstep carrying a pot of soup or stew to add to whatever I might have prepared and stay with us for supper. From time to time, throughout the winter of 1967, all the villagers went to Roger's and Thérèse's house for a *veillée*. Once everyone went down the hill to La Sallette for a *veillée* with the Blevenec family, although Jeanne observed that we would see less and less of them. "Once a family gets the box that talks," she said, "they think they don't need the company of other folks anymore." She was clairvoyant. Soon the age-old reunion would disappear from the Breton landscape; television would be its death blow. Families would lower their blinds and drift into the complacent isolation of self-sufficiency. The box that talks would loosen village ties and extinguish customs that had sustained isolated hamlets for centuries.

On many long and silent evenings, after singing a lullaby to Danielle and tucking her into bed, I would gaze at the night sky, mystified by this ancient village so far removed from anything remotely connected to my past, yet to which

I had become so deeply attached. The reality of my former life had begun to fade as when one dozes on a train and vaguely hears a conductor droning off familiar stops along the way. La Salle had become my only home.

The night the assassination of Martin Luther King was announced on the radio, the anguish of the civil rights movement in the States exploded like a bomb in our kitchen. It can't be! I shouted incredulously at the radio. I turned the dial for more details, but there were none. I drove into Vannes early the next morning to buy the *Herald Tribune* or any other newspaper that might explain what had happened. How and why it had happened. Anything to help me understand.

Speeding along the narrow, winding roads, I remembered the day five years earlier in Paris when Yves' mother had telephoned. "I'm sorry to be the one to tell you the tragic news, Midge," she had said, *"ton président,* Jack Kennedy, *a été assassiné! Il est mort!"*

I remembered dashing down six flights of stairs and running to the nearest kiosk to buy a newspaper. In the street, people were walking as if in a daze. Strangers recognized me as an American and outpoured their sorrow. Shopkeepers who knew me greeted me with tears in their eyes and offered condolences as if a member of my family had died. It seemed that all Paris was in mourning. But now, driving to Vannes, I was alone. I parked my car, bought a newspaper, and went into a café. I scanned through articles, searching for details, eyewitness accounts, anything at all. I longed to share my shock and my sorrow, to feel I belonged to a grieving community, to talk to someone, anyone. But all around me, people were chatting as if nothing had happened or were engrossed in sport sections of local newspapers. I drove back to La Salle. For the first time since I had come to France seven years earlier, I was homesick.

Several months later, Robert Kennedy was killed. I stared in disbelief at my radio. I felt dizzy. What was happening in my country? Had America gone mad? It seemed as if I had lost my way and was wandering through a Salvador Dalí landscape where everything was disconnected and nightmarish. Trying to steady myself, I walked into the courtyard and crossed the road.

Jeanne took me by the arm and led me into the kitchen. "It's terrible, just terrible. Killing that Kennedy boy."

"You heard about it too?" Tears streamed down my cheeks.

"We heard it on Marcel's radio. We were going over to tell you. First that preacher fellow, King, and now another Kennedy boy. It's the way of the world, Mitch. Some people are crazy and want good men dead. There's a lot in this world we can't change."

Marcel walked into the kitchen. He was upset, too. "It's dreadful, all those fine boys getting killed," he said, wiping his tears on his sleeve.

I hugged them both. We sat at the table, and shared what I had read in the newspapers and what Marcel had heard on the radio.

⌒

Assassinations and racial tensions in the States. Student uprisings in Paris. Strikes paralyzing the French economy. All the news from a turbulent world found its way to La Salle, and now that the cocoon had been pierced, nothing could prevent the outside from gushing in. No longer could we shut our eyes to the violence detonating throughout the world. We sat close to our radios, listening. We heard how the war in Vietnam was escalating, how antiwar protests in America were dividing the country. We heard how French police quelled student demonstrators in Paris with tear gas and rubber bullets and how the National Guard killed four innocent students at Kent State University in Ohio. We listened to news of violence spreading throughout France as workers joined student uprisings, and how the once homogeneous French population was becoming shattered and split beyond recognition. Living in a remote country village in the midst of a troubled and explosive world was surreal. Life, on the surface, went on as usual. But things were changing in the country, too. Imperceptibly, yet at breathtaking speed, the ancient way of life in country villages was being thrust, willingly or not, into the twentieth century.

19

Chicken Soup

CLAUDINE WAS ONLY TWELVE, but the shape and grace of her body foretold the woman she would become. She was a young, tall version of Jeanne; her skin glowed, her cheeks blushed from the outdoors, and her mouth drew back easily into a smile. Her eyes sparkled like Jeanne's, and her thick jet black hair fell over her shoulders as Jeanne's must have done before it turned to silver and was pulled back into a bun. Like her grandmother, she was strong and energetic, and a bond of affection was forged between them.

"I couldn't wait to tell you, Mémé," she said breathlessly, bursting into the kitchen. She hugged Jeanne, kissed me on both cheeks, and plopped down on the wooden bench. "It was the middle of the night, and Papa woke me up to help with the birthing. There wasn't even time to get Marcel! I ran to the stable in my nightclothes, and by the time I got there, the calf was half out. He was wet and slippery, and his eyes were shut tight. Mama hadn't got there yet, so I helped Papa pull him all the way out. We laid him down on the ground. Almost right away, it was like he was waking up from a nap. He was trying to stand up! First he straightened out his hind legs. And then his front legs! He was wobbly as if he'd had too much cider. But, *dame*, he was standing. And then he hobbled over to his mother's teats to nurse. Imagine, he'd just been born, but he knew enough to nurse, and he was walking!"

"People say animals are dumb," said Jeanne, nodding. "Why, a calf can do in twenty minutes what the rest of us can hardly do in a year!"

We went on chatting about the birth of the calf and what Claudine was learning in school when the door flew open. Thérèse stood stiffly in the doorway. Her pinched mouth and every muscle in her face were scrunched downward into a scowl.

"Come in, Thérèse, and have a cup of coffee with us," said Jeanne.

Thérèse ignored her. She glared at Claudine. "I knew it. I just knew I'd find you here! The minute I turn my back, you sneak off to your Mémé's house."

"She was just taking a short break from her work, weren't you, Claudine?" said Jeanne.

"Don't take her part like you always do, Mémé," Thérèse snapped. "She'd be sitting around gabbing with you all day if you had your way." She whipped around to face Claudine. "Do you have any idea how much work there is to do? I suppose you expect me to do it all? For all you care, I can wear myself down to the bone 'til I die."

Claudine kept looking down at the floor.

"Please, Thérèse," said Jeanne. "Don't be hard on her. Take a minute to sit and rest with us."

"Stay out of this, Mémé. It's between me and Claudine. As for you, girl, you've had your time off. You'll come with me now if you know what's good for you!" She grabbed Claudine's arm, hustled her outside, and slammed the door behind them.

I had often seen Thérèse ill-humored, but never this angry. I was sure she was jealous of her mother-in-law. Jeanne was outgoing and loved by everyone, whereas Thérèse was sour and withdrawn. To make matters worse, Claudine resembled Jeanne more and more in every way. It must have driven Thérèse crazy, and she showed her resentment of them both at every opportunity.

Jeanne drew back the lace curtain and looked out the window. "Where the blazes is Marcel? He's supposed to whistle when he sees her coming down the path so the poor child can scoot out the back way before Thérèse finds her here."

"So that's why he often looks like he's standing guard outside the house. He's watching out for Thérèse!"

"*Ya.* But he didn't warn us today."

"What was she so angry about?"

"Far as I can tell, she was born angry."

"She can't say Claudine doesn't do enough to help. Everyone knows Claudine works harder than anybody."

"The child works hard all right, but it'll never be enough for Thérèse. On Sundays, the others go visiting, but Claudine has to stay behind to bring in the cows, milk them, feed the pigs, clean the stable, and God knows what else. Now her mother wants her to start working mornings before school at the bakery in Theix. She says twelve is plenty old to go to work. Poor child will have to get up in the middle of the night, ride her bike eight kilometers in all kinds of weather, and shovel heavy loaves into an oven. What's worse is I never heard Thérèse say one kind word to the child. Not once, not even when she was a baby. She's too busy cooing to her pet, Jacqueline." Jeanne stared out the window. "What hurts the most is there's nothing I can do about it. If I say something—anything at all—it's the worse for Claudine."

"I will never understand Thérèse," I said. "She can be friendly and neighborly, like the time she gave us Pierrot. Then the next minute, she barely speaks to me. One day she can be sweet to Danielle when she goes to play with Jacqueline, and a day later, she pushes her away and sends her home in tears. I can't forgive her for that."

"She's always been like that," Jeanne said. "Maybe she'd be different if she didn't hate her life as a peasant."

Jeanne rarely spoke of family problems. She was private, as were all the villagers. If they quarreled with someone, they kept it to themselves. Living in such close proximity, everyone had to get along. Regardless of tensions or long-standing feuds, they greeted one another with four kisses, and when there was a pounding at the door in the middle of the night to help with the birth of a calf, everyone showed up. Still, despite an outward harmony, the same animosities and jealousies as everywhere else simmered under the surface like volcanoes ready to erupt.

"Claudine looks just like you," I said.

Jeanne didn't answer. A sphinxlike expression settled over her face, masking any trace of emotion. She leaned back in her wicker armchair and picked up her basket of knitting. We sat for a while, not talking.

"Something not right's going on in here." Marcel walked in the door. "Never heard you two so quiet."

"Where were you?" said Jeanne, looking up from her knitting. "Thérèse came by, mad as a chicken with its head lopped off. You were supposed to warn us."

"Merde. I screwed up, Mémé. Roger was showing me around his *poulailler*. It'll be the biggest damned henhouse in the Morbihan. Have you seen it, Mitch?"

I had seen the beginnings of a huge and ominous-looking construction behind Roger's farm, fortunately off the road and obscured by trees. Marcel explained that Roger had applied for and received a government loan for a commercial henhouse where they would raise thousands of chickens to sell in nearby towns. "The state's playing Père Noël to us peasants. We'll all get rich," he said. "Isn't that so, Mémé?"

"Just the young ones, not us," murmured Jeanne, engrossed in her knitting.

"She's right, Mitch," said Marcel. "The government wants to push us old folk out of the picture. We grow most everything we eat and we make most everything we wear. We don't buy anything, so they say we're no use to the economy. Now they're telling us we can't kill our own animals or even make our own calvados! Pretty soon they'll pass a law telling Mémé she has to buy her cabbage soup in a tin can from Jean Bonbon. But if we agree to make improvements on the farm, they'll give us money. That's what Roger and Thérèse are doing. You'll see. Pretty soon they'll be rich."

Jeanne looked up from her knitting. "I know peasants in Le Petit Kergaté who got money from the government because they put in indoor plumbing. But then they saw these modern toilet rooms were just the right size and temperature for storing a year's supply of potatoes. They've got the government's pay in their pockets, but you can bet your last *sou* they're in no rush to tear down the old outhouse!" She slapped her thigh and went back to her knitting.

A month later, when the *poulailler* was finished and in operation, Roger took me on a tour.

"We can house ten thousand chickens at a time," he explained proudly, leading me down the main corridor that ran through the center of the huge construction. "Some of 'em are just laying chickens. You've seen the green truck that comes by every other day? That one comes by to pick up the eggs."

"I have," I said. "And a big yellow truck too." My voice changed pitch to talk over the din of the chickens.

"The yellow one comes by every two weeks to deliver new chicks and pick up ones that are ready."

"Ready for *what*?" I shouted, anticipating too well the answer.

"To take them to be killed, packaged, and shipped around to supermarkets," Roger shouted back. "These lights stay on twenty-four hours a day. The chickens never know it's nighttime. They never sleep. They just keep eating, getting fat—and thinking it's time to lay more eggs."

The *poulailler* was an immense honeycomb. There were no windows. Chickens were packed in, jammed against one another, their beaks clattering in incessant shrieking and cackling, their wings flapping in frantic jerking motions, beating against the confines of their cells, their eyes darting about like deranged inmates in an insane asylum. The smell was unbearable, the noise was constant and ear-shattering.

"You'll have plenty of chickens to eat from now on."

"Not these birds," Roger shouted back. "They're sick.

"They're for city people. None of us in the village will ever come near them or their eggs!"

Neither will I, I swore to myself. With the addition of the *poulailler*, Thérèse's and Roger's lives were changing rapidly. As Marcel had predicted, for the first time in their lives, they were making money. They bought a television set, extended the telephone lines across the road, installed a bathroom, and chopped up the outhouse for firewood. Roger bought a tractor, and Thérèse collected magazines for home improvements. Although they continued to eat in the kitchen as they always had, they added a new section to the house that included a living room and a separate dining room for when they had company. Almost overnight, they had modern comforts that peasants had lived without for centuries in both the house and in the fields. Not that there was less work. The whole family had new responsibilities. In addition to working in the fields, Roger handled the business end of the enterprise, organizing pickup and delivery schedules, and keeping records of payments. After school, even Jacqueline began working for the first time, helping her mother in the henhouse. They cleaned the berths, collected eggs that were picked up by the faded green truck every other day, and spilled large burlap bags of chemically souped-up feed into the troughs that ran along each of the rows of cages where the chickens were crammed in. Every two weeks, when I saw the huge egg-yolk-yellow truck drive up the hill past Jeanne's house and park near the *poulailler*, I could imagine too vividly the carting off of fattened and crazed chickens and their replacement with thousands of fluffy, unsuspecting newborn chicks destined for the same incarceration and inglorious ending.

What a contrast to the hearty roosters and hens who

meandered freely in the courtyard at Jeanne and Marcel's farm for four or five months or more, feeding on leftover soups, digging for worms among the pebbles in the courtyard, scurrying out of the way of mobile vendors, cats, or an occasional wild creature sneaking out of the pine woods. Then it struck me. From the moment Yves had ordered me to stop painting, I had been like those crazed pent-up chickens. My cage, while intangible and more ethereal than theirs, had been just as confining, and if I hadn't somehow managed to escape, my spirit would have shriveled with each passing day until it died just as ignominiously as the chickens in the *poulailler*. From that moment on, I looked at Jeanne's chickens romping around the courtyard with different and co-conspiratorial eyes.

Claudine continued working at the bakery and had even more chores on the farm. The older she got, the more beautiful she became, and the worse Thérèse treated her. I thought once Thérèse had acquired modern comforts, she would become less embittered and treat Claudine more kindly. But Jeanne said people don't change because they get more or less money. They stay the same. They keep the character they were born with. I couldn't let myself think what Claudine's life might have been like if her grandmother hadn't lived close by. It saved her. As for me, I couldn't imagine a day going by without Jeanne. Neither Claudine nor I would have survived without her.

20

Cider Country

"I NEVER TOLD YOU ABOUT YANICK?" said Jeanne. "*La pauvre.* The poor child was only twelve when both her parents got killed in an accident. She had no place to go. No relations. So Marcel and me, we took her in. She stayed with us like part of the family for over a year. She hadn't yet turned fourteen when she ran off with a drinking guy who'd gotten her pregnant. I begged her not to go with him. She was too young to listen. Last I heard she's got more kids and lives on a farm near Questembert."

"How long since you've seen her?"

"Seven or eight years since I saw her last. She never came to visit, and Questembert is too far to walk."

"Wouldn't you like to see her again?"

"*Dame, oui.*"

"Listen, we could drive to her farm now. You put on your coif, and I'll finish the dishes."

Jeanne's face lit up. She untied her apron, wrapped it around my waist, and handed me a dishcloth.

"Where's the soap?" I said, looking around.

"Never use it."

"But . . . uh, what about germs?"

"Those things? Never worry about them. The chickens wouldn't like the taste of the dishwater if I used soap." She winked. "They think it's soup."

She went to the cupboard and pulled out the old shoe-box that contained her coifs. Sifting through the neatly folded layers, she picked one out and pinned it on, her deft fingers feeling where the pins should go, reminding me of a pianist's fingers gliding over a keyboard, playing notes known by heart after countless years of practice. "Jean Le Guen. That was the guy's name. We'll have to ask around for his farm."

I finished the dishes, tossed the chickens their soup, and reminded them of the good life they led compared to their poor cousins in the *poulailler*.

⌒

Yanick's farmhouse stood by itself on a barren plot with no trees for shade. Windows were boarded up. Rusted and broken machinery lay where it had fallen, a mangy dog growled at us from the top of a pile of debris, and a few stray chickens pecked around our feet. Except for a clump of dirt that hosted a cluster of bright wildflowers, doggedly refusing to submit to the overwhelming atmosphere of despair, everything about Yanick's house proclaimed "*la misère*." Jeanne's face was drawn and tense as she went to the door. She knocked and called out in an unusually shrill voice, "Anybody home?"

"Come on in. Door's open," came a wooden response.

The house consisted of one spare rectangular room.

The stench of yesterday's food and unwashed diapers was overpowering as we stepped inside. A woman dressed in a torn robe sat in a darkened corner of the room, her hair uncombed.

"Mémé," she said, looking up. "I can't believe it's you. Never thought I'd see you again!"

"I'm still getting around, *ma fille*. This is Mitch, the American lady who lives in our village. She drove me out here to say hello and see how you're doing."

Three young children in tattered clothing eyed us from separate corners of the room. An infant lay naked on an unmade cot, whimpering to itself. Yanick drew herself heavily out of her chair. She was pregnant. She couldn't have been more than twenty, but she looked much older. Although the light in the room was dim, I spotted a fading scar on her cheek and a fresh reddish mark on her neck that retreated under her robe.

"What can I get you both?" she said wearily. "Not that there's much I can offer."

"You needn't bother yourself for us, Yanick child. I brought you some plum jam I put up last fall. I remember you used to like my preserves."

"That's right. It'll be a real treat." She called to the children, "Come over here and give your Mémé a kiss."

Obediently, they shuffled over and stood in line. To each one Jeanne admonished, "You be good to your mother, *mon petit*. She needs you." They returned to their corners, silent and motionless, and like frightened mice stared at the floor, stealing furtive glances at Jeanne and me.

Yanick asked about everyone in the village, one by one, greedily drawing Jeanne out, and for a long while, they reminisced about the year and a half she lived at La Salle. As they talked, lines fell from her face, and when she smiled, she looked like a small child wrapped in the oversize robe of a grown-up.

"You were right all along, Mémé," she said in a small voice.

"No sense in going over that now, child."

"I should have listened to you."

"You were young. You couldn't help it."

"All I'm good for is making babies." She put her hands over her swollen belly.

"Maybe you ought to try not to have any more kids. With four and another on the way, you've got your hands full, that's for sure."

"Yeah. For sure."

Jeanne took Yanick's hands in hers and said, "You stand up strong to your guy, child. You tell him he's a father now. He has to act like one."

"I'll try, Mémé, but there's no talking to him when he drinks." She turned to me with a shy smile. "I'm real glad you came, Mitch. Thanks for bringing her."

"*Kenavo*, child. Anything I can do?" Jeanne asked Yanick, kissing her goodbye on both cheeks.

"No, Mémé, I'll be fine," she answered, the tired and anxious lines rushing back into her face.

We drove off. After a while Jeanne said, almost to herself, "She used to have a pretty face."

"Poor Yanick."

"It's worse than I thought."

"He hits her," I said. "You can see that."

"Probably when he gets himself drunk."

"What can she do?"

"Nothing. What's there to do?"

"Can't she divorce him? I know the Church doesn't allow it, but she can't stay with him."

"Divorce? There's no such thing in the country. And with all those kids, where would she go?"

"It's terrible."

"It's terrible, all right." We drove in silence. Finally she said, "You were the lucky one, Mitch."

"You mean because I could leave Yves when things got bad?"

"That's right."

"When did you know about us?"

"I had a hunch there was trouble the day we went to the beach, you and me. But Yves wasn't a drinker, so I didn't think it would get out of hand. Then that winter, when you and Danielle came to La Salle by yourselves, I knew for sure. I saw bruises on you. Like the ones on Yanick's neck. I cried for you, *ma fille.*"

"I never thought of myself as being lucky. Until now. How horrible it must be to have to stay with someone who hurts you, and know you can never get away."

"God knows it happens in the country. Boys and girls get married before they have a notion of what life's about. Lots of them don't know where babies come from when they marry."

"You were young, too, when you got married, weren't you?"

"Just turned sixteen. But I knew about babies. I helped

with the birthing of five baby sisters and brothers. I figured things out early on."

"I always thought children growing up on a farm knew the facts of life."

"That's not true. Kids grow up watching a bull climb on top of a cow and a calf getting born, but lots of them never put the two together. They see their brothers and sisters being born, they're told it's God's miracle, and they believe it. A girl goes to a church picnic, drinks too much cider, goes out and rolls in a field with a guy. Months later someone tells her she's not sick, she's pregnant, and she has to marry the guy. That's how it was with Yanick. She didn't have any idea what she'd done to get herself pregnant. And I bet neither did he."

"If they don't know how they got pregnant, I suppose they don't know about birth control."

"Birth control? In the country? Listen. Marie Lerinec in Sulniac had a baby every year. By the time she was twenty-four, she had six kids. The last time, they had to cut her open. The doctor told her if she got pregnant again, she'd be dead. She asked the priest what to do. 'Don't wash,' he told her. 'Your husband won't come near you.'"

"That's terrible!"

"Some parents get their kids to be priests or nuns before they're old enough to know what they want in life, before they're old enough to get themselves or anyone else pregnant. That's birth control in the country."

"Your boys didn't become priests."

"I'm glad they didn't. But it's riskier when you have girls. When a girl gets married, she goes from her family farm to his family farm. If she's lucky, they'll treat her fairly.

If they're mean with her or if the guy hits her, that's her bad luck. I had it easy. Luc's family treated me fine and Marcel's a good man. He's got his faults. He drinks too much, but he never gets mean. It's not in his bones. This is apple cider country, Mitch. We make it ourselves, so children start young. Lots of them go straight from mothers' milk to hard cider. Lots of parents give their babies calvados to quiet them down. They quiet down, all right. They pass out. If a kid can't stay awake in school, it's because he had too much cider for breakfast. If a guy drinks, he probably got started as a baby. Like Eric. He's a lost soul. Like Yanick's guy. And now she's stuck with him, poor child, for life."

I shuddered. For life. A life sentence, with no parole. A girl, barely fourteen, pregnant, frightened, off by herself in the woods. A girl locked up in an isolated farm far from a road. No one to call for help. No witnesses. As we sped away from Yanick's prison from which there was no escape, I wondered how many women around the globe were like her, condemned to accept whatever fate dealt them, with no way out, as if they had been tied up, gagged, and led silently to slaughter. And what about Jeanne? She was the most independent woman I had ever known in my life. Surely she would have rebelled if Luc or Marcel had mistreated her. And yet, did I really know her? In a place where there was no divorce, no freedom of choice, where a woman had no options, no recourse regardless of the outcome, would she have resigned herself to being stuck with someone—no matter what—for life? Sometimes I felt I was from a world so far away and so foreign that I would never understand these people I had come to love.

21

Lifting Fog

JEANNE MONTRELAY HAD NEVER VENTURED farther from La Salle than to walk three kilometers across a meadow to go to Mass in Sulniac. The Mass was important to her. It gave her a reason to wear her best coif, to talk to people she saw only on Sundays, to escape the solitude of a farm with three cows, fields with no tractors, no days off, and where the idea of a vacation was unknown. Her needs were minimal. She grew all her vegetables, slaughtered a pig, cured its meat for winter, and made her clothes. In all her life, she had never traveled on a train or ridden on a bus. She didn't own a bicycle. Until we came to La Salle, she had never been in an automobile. Yet, within the confines of her charted world, her life was complete and full. Watching her, I asked myself if I could ever be like her, content to stay on a farm and suppress my restless and insatiable desire to be on the move, to travel, and discover new places.

The Golfe du Morbihan was only eight kilometers from

La Salle. All her life, Jeanne had seen its glimmer at the horizon, but she had never been there. She had never seen its coves, bays, creeks, inlets, rocky beaches, and tiny peninsulas. She had never set foot on one of those peaceful islands that dot the gulf with flowering hamlets hugging the coast, nor the transient, nameless bits of land that emerge every six hours from the sea to serve as temporary resting havens for birds, boats, and fishermen, only to be swept under a returning tide. Jeanne had never been beyond the narrow borders of her small world. Yet, when there was a chance for a new experience, her gray eyes shone more intensely, and a slumbering spirit of adventure awakened in her soul like hot coals reigniting a fire. At times I wondered if, beneath it all, we didn't share the same curiosity for the new and suffer from the same unquenchable wanderlust.

"Danielle and I are going to the gulf today," I said to her, "and Thérèse gave her permission for Jacqueline to come with us. Why don't you join us?"

She shook her head and continued puttering around the fireplace.

"Come with us, Mémé," pleaded Danielle.

"We're going on a boat ride!" exclaimed Jacqueline.

"A boat ride? Well, *mes petites*, if it was maybe before, now it's no for sure."

"Please, Mémé?" implored the girls in unison.

"Listen, everyone," Jeanne said, straightening herself up. "No one on God's earth is going to get me on a boat. Thanks to Mitch here, I went to a beach and got my feet wet. I'm glad I went, but that's as far as I'll go. I was born on land and here's where I'll stay!"

"It's a perfect day," I insisted. "There's no wind. You

wouldn't even know you were on the water. Besides, we'll be back in plenty of time to milk the cows. Please come."

She didn't answer.

"Jeanne darling, you're adventurous, aren't you? We're going to spend the afternoon on Belle-Île. How many times in your life have you had the chance to visit an island?"

She pursed her lips and said nothing.

I pulled back the lace curtains. "Look out the window," I said. "You can almost see it out there. Belle-Île, Jeanne!"

She shrugged. "Belle-Île. Well, I haven't had the chance that many times. I have to admit, Marcel," Jeanne said, turning to him, "I always have been curious about those islands."

"You'll come?"

"She'll come!" cried Danielle.

"Bon voyage," said Marcel, adjusting his glasses. "I figured all along you'd go."

"What about you, Marcel?" I said, propelled by success.

"Not in a hundred years, Mitch. Don't even try."

Jeanne pinned on her coif and said, "All right, *mes filles,* let's get going before I change my mind."

For most of the year, the Morbihan was removed from the tourists' path and remained untouched and unspoiled. But during the month of August, deserted fields and wooded areas that sloped gracefully to the water's edge erupted with mobile homes and bright orange and blue campers' tents like wild chanterelles sprouting up in the meadow beneath La Salle after a spring rain. We drove leisurely along the gulf and past the town of Carnac, where we stopped to walk through a field with rows of ancient, enigmatic forms reaching toward the sky like phantom giants encircling us in their secret domain.

"They're called menhirs," I explained. "No one knows who built them or why, except that they were probably built for religious reasons."

Jeanne nodded knowingly. "Whoever built those things did it to get on the good side of the *curés*. Nowadays we bribe them with our fattest chickens and best cider at Christmas. We peasants will do anything to get a spot in heaven."

We climbed back in the car and continued on to the harbor where boats departed for the islands. As Jeanne stepped onto the gangplank, a sailor recognized her low, pointed coif. *"Bonjour la Morbihanaise!"* he greeted her, smiling, and offering his arm. Nearby passengers turned and waved. She grinned coquettishly and waved back. If she was intimidated by going on her first boat ride, no one would have suspected. The moment the boat left the dock, she strode to the front of the deck, her long black skirt fluttering in the sea breeze, her lace coif securely positioned in her silvery hair, her eyes ablaze. She saw everything, wordlessly devouring the sights of the gulf sparkling in the midmorning sunlight, the jagged coastline, the rocky inlets washed over by waves, and the fresh smell of seaweed that engulfed the boat like breakers rolling up on a beach. She waved at fishermen standing like frozen statues along the dock. She was mesmerized as we gathered speed and left the shore behind, and was entranced as the silhouette of Belle-Île materialized through the mist in the distance. She held tightly to the railing when the ancient harbor, checkered with sea-worn boats of all sizes and colors, came into focus and seagulls dove and soared, filling the salty air with cawing and screeching. Silently she imbibed the whole new dazzling experience.

And for me, all day long, everything appeared more sharply defined, more brilliant and exciting, just as it had been the day we walked together along the beach—as if I were seeing it through her eyes and for the first time.

⁓

"Marcel, you should have been there," she said as we sat down for supper that evening.

"Not me," he said. "You'll never get me on one of those boats."

"It didn't sink, did it? Seeing that island from afar, Marcel, with water all around it, and sailing up to the harbor, with all those boats and houses—each one was a different color—why, I've never seen anything like it. Everywhere you looked there were flowers. And for lunch we had mussels in a place high up where you could watch boats come in and go out to sea.

"Mémé made a really loud noise in the restaurant and everyone heard her," said Danielle, giggling, as Jeanne dug into her pocket for a couple of stowed-away mussel shells, pressed them together at one end, blew into them, and produced a shrill, piercing whistle.

"Well done, Mémé," said Marcel approvingly.

"The restaurant was full of people and noisy," I said, "but when she whistled, even the waitresses stopped what they were doing. People turned to see who made the noise, and when they saw it was Jeanne, everyone applauded and shouted '*Bravo la Morbihanaise!*' "

Jeanne's cheeks flushed a deep russet. She pulled a rumpled handkerchief from her apron pocket, wiped her forehead, and laughed outright. "First time in my seventy-three years I ever went to a restaurant. Wouldn't have missed it for anything. You should have been there, Marcel."

"Mémé, you're happy you went. I'm happy I didn't. Life has a way of working itself out. Let's eat."

⁓

I had never seen light in quite the same way before I came to the Morbihan. I had never been as acutely aware of its subtleties until I lived year-round at La Salle. The more I got to know the region, the more it inspired me. Unlike the mistral-swept, sun-dominated, unequivocally cobalt skies of the Midi, here the sky was rarely constant. Shifting clouds mirrored the ever-changing seascape as the moon-driven tide prevailed upon the waters to rise and sink and follow its whims. Morning light especially took me by surprise. Fog ruled the early hours and clung to the coast until—or if—the sun managed to break through. Morning haze hugged the meadows, emitting a fluid, silvery green light that filtered through the lingering fog, transforming moist fields into shimmering, verdant expanses. Often I awoke early to paint the sunrise. I had painted sunrises before. I had always been drawn to the intense, dramatic impact of sun bursting through night clouds with blazing colors, etching the sky with sharp design. But here, the sun toyed with the morning mist, teasing its way out, blending with the fog in unimagined combinations of delicate shades and hues. Morbihan skies were a continuous display of guile and mystery, seductively revealing and withdrawing their incandescence, gradually unveiling the layered dimensions of their beauty, as if they had to be imagined and coaxed into being.

The weather in the Morbihan was notorious for being cold, damp, and unreliable. Sometimes there were long periods of rain, and summer campers would watch helplessly as their campsites were swept away in sudden downpours. From my hilltop at La Salle, I could watch storms taking shape at the horizon and know that soon I would be whipped by howling winds and inundated, unprotected as if my sturdy stone farmhouses were frail, vulnerable crafts tossed about on high seas. But there were also mild periods throughout the year. Through the clouds and fog, there was always a hint of sun scheming to ease through if only I would wait a little longer. No matter how covered the skies, there was always a spot where the clouds parted to reveal a promise of a brilliant cerulean sky to come.

Each season in the Morbihan unfolded with its own distinctive color scheme. The bright yellow forsythia shrubs and colza fields of April gave way to summer's pastel shades of mauve and lavender heather bushes with sudden, vibrant accents of scarlet poppy fields. When days got shorter, autumn's dazzling palette of copper, rust, ocher, and deep cadmium transformed the landscape as if paint had been splashed about by a wildly undisciplined artist. Like a plant inching its way into the soil, I knew that no matter what happened to me in life, I would always be rooted to this place.

⁓

For more than a year, I had watched Eric cut down the thornbushes. Now I was sure I could do it too. I lowered the moon-shaped machete from its hearth in the garage and went to the path in back of the main house that led into the

woods. It had been weeks since Eric had tended them, and
the briars were sorely in need of trimming. Prickly branches
shot out in all directions like giant claws. Flourishing the
machete like a bullfighter entering the arena to give myself
courage, I imitated Eric's drunken but unerring swing. The
movement felt more natural this time, not jerky and awkward as before. I continued, mystified at the ease with which
I was clipping off the branches. After a while, swinging the
machete no longer felt unfamiliar, and for a moment I had
the odd impression I had been doing it all my life. A superfi-
cial scratch or two appeared on my arms, but nothing compared to the bloody fiasco the first time I faced off with the
briars. As I continued swinging and slicing, my wrist movement became more assured with each blow. While I wasn't
skillful or strong enough to cut through the toughest and
thickest branches, the more slender errant shoots yielded
under my assault and fell submissively to the ground.

Hours later, when I returned the machete to its hook in
the garage, I noticed Yves' old ax resting on a nearby shelf.
"You may be next, *mon ami*," I murmured with a wry smile.
The next day, I returned to the garage, took the ax, and went
to the edge of the meadow near a wooden shed where logs
were stored. It was where Yves had always chopped the
wood. I remembered how I used to stretch out on the grass
to admire his bare torso and sinuous muscles as he balanced
the log on a knotted and twisted stump that from decades of
use had been worn down and scooped out to form the shape
of a Western saddle. He would secure the log in place with
his boot, hurl the ax over his shoulder, and ram it down precisely to the same spot over and over again until, in an
abrupt gesture of capitulation, the log split in two. Sliding a

log onto the stump, I held it in place with my boot as he had done. "Focus on the exact spot where the ax is to strike," I reminded myself. I swung. After coinciding with the log a few times, I noticed with pride a small wedge, making it easier for subsequent strikes to find their mark. I continued. It seemed I had found a rhythm; it was as if Marcel's strength and Jeanne's determination had entered my body, and each stroke followed the last as if I were keeping time with the slow *tick, tick* of an oversize, insistent metronome. As I kept swinging, a sharpened sense of how alone I was enveloped me. Danielle and the other children of the village were in school. The villagers were in the fields. The repetitive sound of the ax pierced the ghostly silence of the countryside, and I stood back to catch my breath. When I started chopping again, it was as if I had stepped out of myself and, from afar, was watching a proud peasant woman from years past, swinging an ax in a never-ending struggle to keep her family warm. A new sense of independence swept over me. No longer was I a poor American woman struggling alone on a farm without a husband. Jeanne was right. I was strong. Although the work that needed to be done was overwhelming, for the most part, I was sure I could do it alone. I would hire Eric to do the work beyond my strength. Otherwise, with all my might, I would manage on my own.

22

To the Rescue

"MOMMY! IT'S DAVID!" I LOOKED up to see the unmistakable freckled face of our old friend from Paris pressed against the window. Pierrot sprang from Danielle's lap, and they ran outside and leaped into his outstretched arms.

I threw open the window and called to him. "David! What on earth are you doing at La Salle?"

"Come to see you, my beauties."

"I thought you were in Calcutta."

"True, I was. I'll tell you about that later. But in a word, I had to cut short my trip. And I thought, now wouldn't it be nice to pay a visit to my favorite lassies in the whole world? So I came."

"On foot?"

"Not quite."

"Where's your car?"

"The Blue Goddess lies in distress at the bottom of the hill."

"Your MG broke down?"

"Only reluctantly. She almost made it. But this last hill was more than she could muster."

"She's not a youngster anymore."

"True. I tried pushing her, but I picked up some kind of bug in Calcutta. I'm perfectly well now but still a bit shaky."

"You do look rather emaciated. Come inside." Danielle grabbed his arm and pulled him into the house. "We're having dinner in a little while," I said. "We'll start building you up."

"Just like the old days in Paris."

"I seem to remember you always did arrive just in time to eat."

"Oh, that. Pure chance."

"Good timing."

"Listen, my love. I hate changing subjects. Especially about food. But is there anyone around here strong enough to help me push a sick car up the hill?"

"I am!" said Danielle brightly.

"So am I," I said, "but we'd better get Roger to help. He lives across the road."

On the way, I introduced David to Jeanne and Marcel, and they offered to help. Roger, Thérèse, Jacqueline, and Claudine were in the stable and leaned out from under the cows they were milking. "Give us a few minutes, and we'll give you a hand," said Roger. When they finished, we all headed down the hill. Off the road near La Sallette, Monsieur Blevenec and his son Jean were examining the stalled car.

"Look at this dashboard," said Jean admiringly. "It's a sports car, isn't it?" David nodded modestly.

"It's a real bright blue, David," said Monsieur Blevenec, running his palm along the hood.

"I painted it myself," said David, tapping the roof.

"I've never seen a car this bright a color," said Roger. "You sure can't miss it coming down the road."

Jeanne broke in. "Listen. Let's get to work. You guys can talk about what a pretty blue it is after we've pushed this bastard up the hill."

Madame Blevenec; her four daughters, Huguette, Jeannine, Yolande, and Monique; and her father, Monsieur Allanic, who by now was hard of hearing and got around with the help of a walking stick, came out of the house to see what the excitement was about. Everyone milled about and, except for the old man, got in position to push the car. Surrounded by the entire village, first by inches, then by starts and lurches, the car began its uncertain odyssey up the hill. All the while, David followed behind, looking like a disheveled movie director, gesturing wildly and shouting directions: "*À gauche*, that's it. No, too much. *À droite!*"

Finally, the Blue Goddess made it up the hill and was positioned statuesquely in the courtyard, in front of the stable. We congratulated ourselves. Everyone admired the car, and the villagers ambled back to their farms.

"She may be a work of art," said David, "but will she ever make it back on the road?"

"You're an expert mechanic. You'll have her running in no time."

"Maybe. Maybe not. I'll need parts that might be a bit tricky to find in this part of the world. You could have me on your hands for a while."

"I want you to stay always," Danielle blurted, gazing at him adoringly.

From under the hood, he turned his head to her and

smiled. "If I can't get this bloody car to start, you may have your wish, my little darling."

After supper, David kept us spellbound with stories of his trip to Calcutta, how he helped bring food to remote villages where famine was rampant and children were starving, how he dug wells and built roads in faraway places where the drought was the worst and where roads didn't exist, and how he was attacked by local villagers who didn't understand that he had come to help them, and since he didn't speak their language, he couldn't explain to them why he was there. He enchanted Danielle with a Scottish lullaby when it was time to put her to bed, and after she'd gone to sleep, we went outside and sat under the stars.

"I saw Yves before I left Paris," David said, pouring me a glass of cider. "He said to say hello."

"I used to think there was a chance for us. But not anymore."

"That's not what he says. He says you belong together. That it might take time, but you'll work things out. I think you will, too."

I held up my glass to his. "Dream on, my friend," I said. We clinked.

"Change of subject, Midge." He grimaced. "I have a confession."

"I love confessions. What have you been up to?"

"I hate to admit it, but I'm broke. I can't even pay the rent for the hovel in Paris I sleep in. So I thought . . . well, maybe I could stay on at La Salle for a little while and help out with the garden and the chores . . . That is, if you have room . . ."

"Room? Have you looked around? We have half a hamlet! It's a brilliant idea. Have some more cider."

On the spot, we decided that David would send for his painting materials and move into La Salle. In exchange, he would help in the garden and with repairs around the house. Danielle would be thrilled. From the time we knew him in Paris, it seemed he was a member of the family. There was endless work to be done, and although I wanted to prove to myself and to everyone else that I could handle it alone, I was thankful to have help. The arrangement appealed to me enormously.

David slept in the guest room adjacent to my room that night. Around two o'clock in the morning, I was awakened by strange noises. It sounded as if David were gasping for air and moaning. I called to him through the closed door, "David, are you all right?" No answer. I called again. Finally I opened the door and found him nearly unconscious, feverish, and dripping with sweat. "Can you hear me, David?" I said, lifting him by his shoulders and trying to revive him. He didn't respond. His eyes were half open, but he didn't seem to see me. I put him down gently. I ran to the kitchen to telephone Dr. Le Cam. Although it was the middle of the night, he must have heard in my voice how frightened I was. He told me to keep calm and describe David's symptoms.

"Cover him with a blanket," he instructed. "Put cold compresses on him to bring down the fever. Can you bring him to me right away?"

I wrapped a blanket around David as best I could and put a cold washcloth over his forehead. I ran to Jeanne's house and called up to the tiny darkened window in the attic over the kitchen.

"Jeanne! Mémé! Wake up, please."

I called again, louder. A dim light lit up the window. A voice called down, "What is it, Mitch?"

"I'm taking David to the doctor. He's terribly sick."

Moments later, she appeared at the front door in a long woolen nightgown and carrying a knit shawl. Silhouetted by the blackness of the night illuminated only by stars, her long silvery hair streamed down her back like the sudden downpour of a spring shower, and the night light flickered around her as if fireflies followed her as she moved. "Can you stay with Danielle?" I asked.

With a quick gesture, she whipped the shawl around her shoulders. "Let's go," she said, and we rushed across the road. David was lying where I had left him, sweating, shivering, and he seemed to be hallucinating. Jeanne helped me get him into the backseat of the car. She watched us drive away and then turned to go in the house. The image of her standing at the front door stayed vividly in my mind as I drove as fast as I could to Vannes. I had never before seen her with her hair undone.

Dr. Le Cam was waiting for us. We managed to get David into his office. I went into the foyer and waited, wondering if he would survive. I had never seen anyone that sick. His skin had become ashen gray, purplish circles around his eyes made his face look like a death mask, and his red hair looked wild and ghoulish and swirled around him. His breathing had become more of a wheeze, and he was shaking uncontrollably. Oh, David, I thought in despair. You went to India to help starving children, and now you're going to die so young.

After what felt like hours, Dr. Le Cam came into the foyer.

"He should be all right, Midge. You got him here in time. I gave him an injection, so he'll be groggy for a while. All of us are lucky I had experience with these diseases during the war. I'm probably the only doctor in the Morbihan to have heard about them. Someone else might have treated him for a bad case of the flu and we would have lost him."

"What's the matter with him?" I asked.

"You told me he was in Calcutta?"

"He went there to help famine and drought victims."

"He must have picked up a nasty strain of malaria while he was there. Probably didn't have the best hygiene. I treated him with what I have on hand and wired Paris for medication. I'll bring it out to La Salle as soon as it arrives. We need to watch for a relapse, but he should recover. We can put him back in the car now."

David did recover. After a few weeks, he was sitting up and showing signs of his animated, puckish self again. Convinced that the combination of his car breaking down and his nearly dying was an indisputable omen that he was meant to stay on at La Salle, we transferred his few belongings from the guest room to the temporary house, which instantly became "David's house." Danielle was overjoyed. "David's my big brother," she said, and by way of confirmation he picked her up with his remaining strength and swung her around, shouting weakly, "Whoopee! I have a little sister!"

23

Unfinished Business

JEANNE PUT IT SUCCINCTLY: we now had another mouth to feed. Neither David nor I had any noticeable income, and neither our separate nor combined bank accounts held any promise for the future. True, living expenses were minimal in the country. I paid no rent. La Salle was an agricultural property; taxes were less than ninety dollars a year. We lived off fruits and vegetables from our garden. Jeanne provided us with eggs, chickens, and an occasional rabbit for which we paid next to nothing. Still, there were the unavoidable expenses: groceries, car insurance payments, gasoline, and clothes for Danielle, who, vying with the tomato plants, shot up an inch or two every time I blinked. Health care, fortunately, was not a problem. Doctors and dentists in Vannes accepted paintings in exchange for services, a bartering custom then common in the Morbihan. When Dr. Bonnefous removed Danielle's tonsils, Madame Bonnefous picked out a watercolor seascape I had done of boats mooring in the harbor at twilight. After Dr. Le Cam finished treating David's Calcutta crisis, his wife came to La Salle and sat for a portrait. The most predictable and dreaded expenses—for which there was no bartering—occurred after the frequent wind- and rainstorms ripped through La Salle, pounding the sturdy buildings, wrenching the blue-black slates off seven roofs, and sending them crashing to the ground for redundant dramatic effect. When my father sent money for La Salle, he stipulated that ownership of the hamlet be put in my name. I didn't think it mattered then. But now, I was grateful. Yves, in parting, had made it clear I could never ask him for financial help. He reasoned that a genius must never be burdened with mundane family responsibilities. So it was up to me to figure out how to make money in a remote hamlet in the middle of the Morbihan.

Soon after David's recovery, Noël and Jacques Le Brusque came to dinner. I invited Jeanne and Marcel to join us. Jeanne brought a *quatre quarts,* still warm from the oven, and Marcel brought two bottles of their best sparkling cider. During the usual tour through the buildings, we stopped in the stable. Looking around, Jacques stroked his beard and observed dreamily, "Can't you imagine a show of our paintings here?"

"It would be fabulous!" exclaimed David.

"You can't hang paintings on these walls. They're filthy," said Noël, who had a tendency to ground fantasies.

"A good scrub will fix that," injected Jeanne matter-of-factly.

We all turned to her. "And then we could paint them," added Jacques, "and figure out a way of lighting the work."

"Be realistic, *mes chers*," said Noël. "You'd be wasting

your time. Who would come to see paintings in the middle of nowhere? And more to the point, who would buy?"

"Look," countered Jacques. "There isn't an art gallery in Vannes or within a radius of fifty kilometers. If we publicized it, people would come, even if just out of curiosity."

"And once they got here, they might buy," said David.

"Now you're talking sense," said Jeanne, nodding approvingly.

"We should appoint Jeanne as director of the gallery," I said, kissing her on the cheek.

"Great idea," said Jacques. "And we'll ask the Rotary Club of Vannes to sponsor us."

"Fantastic!" effused David, "Then we'd be respectable and the whole of the Morbihan would come to see it."

"Well, if the Rotary Club got involved . . ." said Noël, wavering.

"Marcel," said Jeanne with a satisfied grin, "looks like you and I are going to see our first picture show."

The idea had taken root. We contacted the local office of the Club Rotary de Bretagne. Always on the lookout for worthy causes, they embraced the idea, formed an art committee to oversee the project, and began meeting at La Salle on a regular basis to plan the show. We invited other painters and sculptors we knew to join us. With seven houses, we had more than enough space to put them up for seven or eight days. I had long dreamed of turning La Salle into an art community; now it would become one, if only for a week. Jacques contacted a painter of still lifes and figures named Jean-Pierre from the town of Laval. Andres, a German sculptor I knew, lived in the country in the southwestern part of France. He worked with the traditional methods of blacksmiths and made powerful wrought-iron sculptures. Andres would surely come. I wrote to a friend in the north of Brittany who researched the recipes of old masters, made his own paints, and painted jewel-like whimsical scenes of fantasy. Moarche answered saying he would join us. The Rotary Club offered to pay for the artists' transportation, arrange for local newspaper advertising and radio publicity, and supply wine and fruit juice for the vernissage. Throughout the winter months, plans for the show mushroomed.

One afternoon, a young Spanish woman named Mosca appeared at La Salle. Brusque, with strong features and a piercing gaze, she had heard about an upcoming exhibition and came to show us examples of her work. But something about her manner troubled me. It wasn't that she was aggressive. An artist had to be pushy sometimes so that people would pay attention. But there was something caustic, even sinister, about her manner. When she went out to the car to get her paintings, I told David about my reservations.

He laughed. "She's a strong woman, but that shouldn't scare us off, Midge. Let's see what she does."

Mosca's paintings were a series of disturbing stark figures that all looked like her. David raved about her work, and I admitted that they were powerful. We opened a bottle of cider, and as we toasted the upcoming show, she relaxed and became friendly, and I began to regret my negative first impression. In the end, I agreed with David that she would be an exciting addition to the group. Mosca was included in the show.

One day, as I was washing up the kitchen and David was

putting away the dishes, he said, "Wouldn't it be great if Yves showed his work with us in the show? Why don't we invite him?"

Yves? Here? A part of the exhibition? It was as if David had struck me with an iron club. By now, I felt I had weathered the separation and was coming into my own. Except for rare moments, I steadfastly refused to admit how devastating the breakup had been for me. For Danielle's sake, I had to be positive and strong. Long ago, Jeanne had told me that with all the work on the farm and raising her boys, she didn't have time to think about being sad or lonely. It wasn't quite the same for me, but the demands of maintaining a vegetable garden, keeping rapacious thornbushes in check, chopping firewood, caring for seven buildings and seven and a half acres of land, and raising a precocious seven-year-old kept me from dwelling too much on the past.

Without Jeanne, I could never have managed. She rescued my garden, which otherwise would have mutated into a weed-infested jungle. Now it provided vegetables for Danielle, David, me, and anyone who stopped by for supper. She brought Moomoot, Cocotte, and La Petite Belle to our side of the road to munch on the grass whenever it grew too high. She kept my spirits from sinking into the depths of discouragement; she gave me courage to confront challenges I never knew existed. Thanks to her, La Salle was thriving. The restoration of the main houses had been successful beyond my hopes. And now, with the art show, hopefully we would make enough money to cover roof repairs for the foreseeable future. But if Yves were to come to La Salle now, everything I had struggled to accomplish would be put on display for him to judge and criticize. He would be furious I had gone back to painting. He would demolish everything.

"David thinks we should invite Yves to be in the show," I said to Jeanne the next day over coffee. "He says it wouldn't be right to have an exhibition and not ask him to be a part of it."

She took my hand in hers. "What do you think, Mitch? Do you want to see him?"

"Not after his last visit, but I don't know what to do. Danielle needs to see her father. I wouldn't be here at La Salle if not for him. I'm grateful to him for that. Still, I'm frightened, Jeanne. If he were to come, and if he became violent, it would turn everything I've accomplished into a nightmare."

"With lots of people around, it's safe enough, but don't you make a decision until you feel sure what's right for you. Whatever you decide, don't you worry. You're among friends now."

After a week, I called him.

"Hello, Yves? It's Midge."

There was silence.

"I called to tell you we're having an art show at La Salle. If you're interested, we'd like you to show your paintings with us. Besides, Danielle would be so glad to see you."

"An art show? Who's exhibiting?"

"Jacques Le Brusque, David, some friends, and me."

"Who would come to see it?"

"We've had a lot of publicity. People from Vannes and other nearby towns."

He said he would think about it. He asked about Danielle, and we said goodbye.

In April, the artists arrived. We were seven in all: Jacques, David, Andres, Jean-Pierre, Moarche, Mosca, and me. Mosca carved a woodcut of austere geometric figures that we printed as a poster and tacked up in shops and on trees around nearby towns and villages. Jeanne and Marcel pitched in with everyone else to clean, polish, and paint the stable. Jeanne was curious about each piece as we hung the artwork. "Who did it?" she would ask. "How did he make it? What's it about?" She asked about all of them—except one, a reclining nude by Jean-Pierre. It was a large, spare painting, with the model propped up on her elbow, reminiscent of Goya's Duchess of Alba, staring frankly and immodestly at the viewer. Knowing how foreign any kind of nudity was for people in the country—Jeanne told me that wives never undressed before their husbands—I had been hesitant about hanging the nude for fear of offending the villagers. But in the end, we decided it was a beautiful painting and should be included.

After a week of nonstop cleaning, painting, and installing lights, the stable was transformed into a professional albeit rustic gallery, with an uneven cement floor, cavernous ceilings, and massive rusting hooks that not long ago had fastened cows to their stalls and now were interspersed among works of art. Each painter had space for four, five, or six paintings, and Andres' forceful iron sculptures stood dramatically in the center of the enormous showroom.

Over coffee the next morning, Jeanne said, "Everyone in the village is excited. In all my life, I never saw so many people coming and going to La Salle."

"It's only for a little while longer," I said to reassure her. "After the show, the artists will go back home, and the village will go back to normal. I promise."

She tapped her fist on the table. "Mitch, I've had nearly seventy-five years of peace and quiet. It's about time we had some commotion around here. With all this art stuff, we're going to put La Salle on the map!"

The day of the exhibition arrived. Shortly before it was scheduled to begin, around noon, Yves drove the Deux Chevaux up the hill and parked alongside the vegetable garden. At first, I didn't see him. Then I heard Danielle call to him. To my surprise, I felt strangely calm and greeted him as if I had seen him the day before.

"Curiosity got the best of me," he said, kissing me on the cheek. Danielle and David rushed to him, embraced him, and we introduced him to the other artists. Everyone followed him around the stable as he appraised the work. An urgent call to the kitchen rescued me before he arrived at my paintings; thus I escaped witnessing his reaction to my recent work.

Unending lines of cars traveled up the hill to La Salle. The Rotary Club of Vannes had touted the show to all their regional clubs. Journalists and photographers came to interview the artists and photograph works of art at the new Centre d'Art de La Salle. Local newspapers had publicized the first art show in the countryside of the Morbihan, bringing people from towns eighty kilometers away, as far as Quimper and Rennes.

Jeanne said the artwork had performed a miracle because in all her years, she had never seen so many people come together. Marcel, Roger, Thérèse, their daughters, and the Blevenecs and their five children came. Jeanne's younger son Marcel, his wife, the other Thérèse, and their children came. Villagers from Locqueltas, Trévégan, and Kerlomen came. The priest from Sulniac came, along with the nuns from the school where most of the children from La Salle and nearby villages attended. Peasants I didn't know by name, but whom I had passed by and waved to in fields, came. It was the first art exhibition the local people had ever seen. Mingling with peasants dressed in Sunday suits and white starched coifs, city people and townspeople from all around poured into La Salle. They pointed to David's dream-like oil pastel landscapes, some were familiar with my paintings of the surrounding countryside and gulf, and now they were discovering the works of other artists. Danielle didn't know if she was more ecstatic to see her father or to see so many people. She greeted everyone and led them by the hand to the stable. After explaining breathlessly that her mother's and David's paintings were in the show, she skipped back to kiss her father and then ran to the gate to greet the next wave of people. Jeanne was a perfect guide. She escorted the priest, the nuns, and all the peasants she knew from Sulniac and nearby farms, proudly pointing out who the artist was and how the painting was done.

"See those pieces of iron over there?" she said. "Andres, that German fellow over there, made them. He works like Émile, the *forgeron* in Theix. That picture over there? Moarche, the skinny one, did it. He makes the colors himself. Grinds them down from a piece of rock 'til he has a mound of powder. Mixes it with the same cooking oil I put in salads. He showed me how he does it. They all know what they're doing. That's for sure."

For every painting, she had something to say, but when she came to Jean-Pierre's impudent nude, the one painting that made all the villagers avert their eyes, she tilted her head to indicate it and passed it by with a wink, but not a word.

Yves and I had hardly spoken. As I watched him standing alone across the courtyard, a feeling of indescribable sadness overcame me. His face had changed. His expression had hardened, and I could see only faint traces of the man I had loved so dearly. This man, who from the first epitomized everything I found sensitive, masculine, and appealing, now stood apart like an outsider, enclosed upon himself. I started to turn away when suddenly my sadness transformed into fury, and I felt angrier than I had ever been before. What right did he have to change? How dare he no longer be the man I trusted, the man on whom I counted to share this life, this house, these pine woods, these precious bonds with the villagers, and this endearing child, who was growing and blossoming far removed from his sight and affection. What right did he have to deny us the chance to produce art in this incomparable place that he alone had discovered and had believed in? Accusations and recriminations spun around my head, and I fought back tears of rage and heartbreak. I couldn't look at him. Quickly I turned away and lost myself in the crowds of people milling around the courtyard and stable.

Later in the afternoon, he approached me without my noticing and slipped his arm through mine. "I have to admit, you and your friends certainly succeeded in getting people to come see the show."

"The Rotary Club got the word around," I said, steadying my voice. "It's good you came. It's important for Danielle."

"We need to talk," he said. He led me away from the

exhibition toward the cider house, once again my studio. Leaving the crowds behind, he said quietly and earnestly, "I've been thinking, Midge. Maybe there is a way you and I could get back together."

How strange. The words I had hoped to hear for so long had no meaning for me now. We passed through the stones he had sculpted around the doorway of me singing "Old Man River" and went inside, where the walls were alive with sketches tacked up and large, colorful, exuberant paint-ings leaning against the walls. One painting was unfinished. It was huge, the largest painting I had ever attempted. It was an oil painting of low tide at a beach. I had painted it at the gulf, but it could have been a beach anywhere in the world, anywhere you could be standing alone on an endless beach and feel the hypnotic pull of the tide, beckoning you to risk the unknown, to venture into an uncertain future, to allow yourself to be carried out to sea.

"Listen, Mijoux," he said. How long had it been since I had been called Mijoux? "Marriage—I mean the way we lived together before—was wrong for us. If we get back to-gether, it has to be different. Something completely new. Don't you agree?"

I listened.

"You see, traditional marriage doesn't work anymore— not for artists like you and me. For people like us, it has to be reinvented. It can't keep trying to stand on the same tired legs it's been limping around on for centuries. It needs to be reinvigorated. Become something new and bold."

I looked into his eyes. He always did have unconven-tional ideas; I had admired him for that. We sat across from each other at my worktable, which was crowded with sketch pads, paints, and oversize tin cans crammed with brushes and palette knives.

"I've given this a lot of thought over the past few years," he went on, becoming more animated. "I think I've come up with a solution. Listen: you and Danielle will come back to Paris. Not to my apartment, of course. Married people shouldn't live under the same roof. That's the old way. You'll sell La Salle, and the money you'll get for it will set you and Danielle up in your own apartment. You'll stop painting, of course, and get a full-time job. That way you'll be able to support yourself and Danielle. We'll live independently, and the most essential part of the arrangement is that you will never ask me for anything. Especially money. We'll have separate lives, and see each other whenever my work permits. That way it can work out for us. I know it can. Don't you see? Traditional marriage is doomed. It can't help but fail, especially for creative people. But if we follow the blueprint I've worked out, we'll have another chance. We can have a life together."

As I listened to him, conflicting reactions clamored for my attention. In spite of the fact that he had canceled out my life as a painter with one brash stroke, as well as produced the most pragmatic, least romantic proposal in history, I was moved. In his own way, Yves, over the years of our separation, had been searching for a remedy. Perhaps it was the only arrangement that would work for him, but for me, his words struck strident chords. The man he had become was not the man I once loved. Somewhere along the way, the tender poet, the man who thrilled and inspired me, the ardent lover whom I loved so much had died. Someone for whom I had no feeling sat across from me. He hugged me as we left the cider house;

it was as if a stranger was holding me. I told him I would think about it. Should I have told him at that moment, face-to-face, that there could never be a reconciliation between us? That I could never recover the love I once felt for him? Was I still fearful of his sickness, of his erratic behavior? Later that evening, with a wistful feeling as if for a lost friend, I watched him leave again, and for the last time.

The reception to the exhibition was beyond our expectations, although sales were modest. I sold several watercolors. Moarche sold two small paintings. Jacques sold a few sketches, and Jean-Pierre sold a still life. Andres took commissions for wrought-iron chandeliers he made to meet expenses, and David fell in love with Mosca.

24

La Misère

"Just like a rabbit," Jeanne used to say. "Always scratching at the cage. Can't stay in one place." Whenever I sped off in the camionette, she watched from her doorstep and listened anxiously for my return. She would cross the road and greet me with kisses on both cheeks, and then shake her head and scold, "Don't you know it's dangerous to be on the road?" I dismissed her concern until I remembered she had lived her entire life far removed from the frenetic pace of trains, planes, and superhighways. To her, every time I drove my car to Vannes to do the marketing, to spend an afternoon exploring the gulf, to search for a rocky beach where I hadn't yet gone swimming or an inlet I hadn't sketched before, I was risking my life.

One day I announced to her as gently as possible, "Danielle and I are going to Chicago to visit my parents."

"What!" She glowered. "That's halfway around the world. I suppose you'll be flying in one of those devilish air machines over the ocean?"

"You worry too much, Jeanne darling," I said. "It's perfectly safe. Besides, we'll only be away for three weeks, and David will take good care of Pierrot and the garden. We'll be back before you even notice we're gone."

⌒

It was the winter of 1970. Ten years had gone by since I left for Paris to paint. When I boarded the *Queen Elizabeth* in 1960, America was still wedded to the lifestyles and attitudes of the fifties. Returning a decade later, I assumed I would find the country unchanged. But while I had been planting potatoes and pulling weeds in a remote hamlet in Brittany, the United States experienced three assassinations, the acceleration of the Vietnam War, the polarizing of generations and races, and the tearing apart of a population to a degree unknown since the Civil War. People talked of racial uprisings. Friends cautioned me against driving through Chicago's all-black neighborhoods, where they said whites were ambushed and attacked. Discussions about the war in Vietnam turned ugly, people were tense and defensive. Families were split. Drugs were rampant. Crime was on the rise. America was like a patient in a state of shock, so traumatized by tragic events, one after another, that it was no longer possible to snap back to a normal state. I had followed many of these events from afar, gleaning what I could from newspapers and the radio. But I couldn't possibly have known how wrenching it was to live through them firsthand. I felt like a foreigner. I had been speaking French for ten years; my English was rusty. My thoughts and dreams were in French. Often I searched for a word, translating the French into English. People said to me, "How well you speak English. Where did you learn?" I wondered if I had been away from my country so long and during such crucial years that I would never be able to feel at home there again.

The trip, however, served its purpose. My parents had longed to see their grandchild and know her as she was growing up. They embraced Danielle with stored-up affection. After having lived much of her young life with too small a family, she was now surrounded by adoring grandparents, uncles, aunts, and cousins. At seven, she spoke English with a French accent, enchanting family and strangers alike. My mother couldn't spoil her enough. My father lavished affection on her and vowed to visit La Salle. Each minute was precious, intensified by the brevity of our stay. The weeks flew by, and because of a mix-up in dates, we returned a day earlier than expected.

"Won't David be surprised!" said Danielle eagerly. But driving into the courtyard at La Salle, I felt uneasy. Everything looked oddly neglected, abandoned.

"Pierrot! Pierrot!" called Danielle, hopping out of the car. "Mommy, where's Pierrot?"

"I don't know, darlingette. I expected a big welcome from him, too."

We went to open the door, but the silent language of the house warned me not to enter. "We won't go inside just yet," I said. We turned and crossed the road.

"Mitch! You're back! Thank goodness." Jeanne reached out her arms to embrace us. But her face was tense, and Marcel looked down and shook his head.

"What's going on? Jeanne. Marcel. What is it?"

"Where's Pierrot?" asked Danielle.

"You tell her, Mémé," said Marcel.

"Tell her what?" I asked.

Jeanne took Danielle's hand. "Sit here by me, *ma petite*. It happened a week after you and your mother left."

"Where's my Pierrot?"

"Pierrot got run over, Danielle."

"Where is he? Is he hurt?"

"I don't know how, but I have to tell you. He was killed."

Danielle burst into tears.

"Marcel and me, we buried him." Jeanne put her arm around her. "I'll take you to his grave this afternoon."

"How did it happen?" I asked.

"It's terrible what's been going on, Mitch," said Marcel, pounding his fist on the table.

"The day you left, Mosca moved in with David," said Jeanne. "It was the worst thing that could have happened. He hasn't been the same since. And then that architect fellow from Vannes started coming around."

"You don't mean Guerain?"

"That's him," said Marcel. "The one with boots and a big black car. He's been coming all right, with that girlfriend of his."

"And not just them," added Jeanne. "They had parties every night. Cars coming and going. That's when Pierrot got run over. Some of them were good and drunk."

"Pierrot was trying to keep them out," I said, trying to comfort Danielle.

"He was . . . a good watchdog," she struggled to say through her sobbing.

"Those people, we could hear them all night long from across the road," Jeanne went on. "They were still at it when

I got up to milk the cows. And David. He gets sick in the head when Mosca is around. I tried and tried to talk to him, shake some sense into him, but he wouldn't listen. Every day, it got worse. I never saw anything like it. They trashed everything."

Together with Jeanne and Marcel, we walked back across the road. Neglected as the courtyard and vegetable garden were, it wasn't until we walked into the kitchen that we saw the extent of the damage. Everything in sight was broken or burned. Empty bottles of cider, wine, and gin were everywhere, ashtrays overflowed, chairs were overturned. Mosca's drawings were tacked on the walls. Not the strong, stark drawings she had shown in the art show, but angry, explicit sexual drawings that I kept ripping off before either Jeanne or Danielle could notice them or take a closer look.

Unwashed dishes were piled up in the sink. Garbage in and out of trash bags was everywhere. Dirty pots and pans sat on the stove, encrusted with food and charred on the bottom. The cupboard with jams, dried fruit, boxes of cookies, and extra canned goods had been razed. We crossed through the corridor to the bedrooms. The bathroom was filthy. In Danielle's room, the guest room, and my room, clothes were strewn around, beds unmade. David had his own house. Had he and Mosca moved into the main house? Had Guerain slept in my bed? I couldn't let myself think about that. All I wanted to do was clean, repair, and fumigate the house. La Salle had been vandalized and violated. I was heartsick.

"I couldn't warn you," said Jeanne, her eyes brimming over with tears. "For the first time in my life, I wished I knew how to write. I wanted to write you a letter. I couldn't do anything but sit back and watch their goings-on."

"Even if you had written me, Mémé darling, what could I have done from Chicago? There was nothing any of us could have done." I put my arm around her, and she wiped her tears with her apron.

In the cupboard, we found a few remaining tea bags. We scrubbed a pot and boiled water.

"Are you angry at David?" asked Danielle anxiously.

"Very."

"Are you going to punish him?"

"All these years I thought of him as a kid brother. I thought he was gentle. Maybe he is. But he's weak. He's a chameleon who changes colors and blends in with his surroundings. He's influenced by whoever he's with. For good or for bad."

"Mosca is bad for him, for sure," Jeanne said. "But it was up to him to stop this from happening."

I stared into my teacup. "It's like your story about old man Fotreau. David promised to help, but he made everything worse. He turned into the sonofabitch nephew!"

"Don't you worry, Mitch," said Jeanne. "Marcel and I will help fix it up."

"I'll help too, Mommy. Don't be angry with David. It's not his fault that Pierrot is dead," pleaded Danielle, her cheeks stained with tears.

Minutes later, Guerain's Mercedes roared into the courtyard. He must have seen our camionette. We heard him spin his car around, gun the motor, and speed down the hill.

A moment later, David and Mosca burst in.

"Hi, my loves! What a surprise! Didn't expect you 'til tomorrow." David rushed to us with his usual panache, but his cheeks were flushed and he was ill at ease. Mosca followed close behind him; her face was blank, indifferent. Yet the brilliance in her eyes gave the impression she was reveling in the awkwardness of the situation. David went on, "Danielle, my little darling. Give me a hug. I'm sorry about Pierrot, honestly I am. It was awful. I'll get you another pup, little sis, you'll see. Look, Midge, don't worry about the mess; I'll have it cleaned up in no time. Just didn't have time. How was your trip?"

"David." I stared him in the eye, my face revealing the depth of my disappointment. "There's no point in pretending. The house is in shambles. So is the garden. But worse, you allowed Guerain and his friends to come to La Salle, maybe even stay here and sleep here, knowing who he is and how I feel about him."

"I know it looks bad. But I can explain . . ."

"We had a few parties, Midge," said Mosca, edging close to me. "No harm in that. You always liked a good party."

I couldn't look at her. She was a poisonous viper coiled under a rock, waiting to strike. I turned to David. "I trusted you. With the house. The garden. With Pierrot. With everything. You were a part of our family. How could you let me down like this?"

"Listen, Midge, I can explain . . ."

"We're going to Jeanne's house. When we come back, I want you both gone." Danielle burst into tears again.

An hour later, we heard David's MG drive off. I knew I could never be friends with him again.

⌒

The following morning, the two gendarmes from Elven drove up the hill and parked alongside the entrance to the courtyard. Jeanne and Marcel came to the road.

"What brings you boys to La Salle?" said Jeanne, peering inside the car.

"We're following up on a lead about the architect Guerain, Mémé. Sorry to bother you, Madame Drumont," said the bald one, climbing out of their tiny car. "We got word that arms and explosives might be hidden on your property."

"Arms? Explosives?"

"Yes, ma'am. We suspected for a long time that Guerain was a part of the Breton Libre movement," he said. "We couldn't prove it. But lately we've gotten hold of solid evidence against him. Sorry, but we've got to search the whole place."

"Guerain was our architect for a short time," I said. "We got rid of him when we found out he'd been a collaborator. I'll help you with the search."

"What did David do?" asked Danielle in a small voice.

"Maybe the little one should stay in the house, Madame Drumont," said one of the gendarmes. "It could be dangerous."

"You stay here with me, Danielle," said Jeanne, putting her arm around her.

Marcel and I went from house to house with the policemen as they combed the attics, pried open boxes, and inspected each carton or container, wherever arms might have been hidden. In my studio, I pointed to a trapdoor that led to the cave where Monsieur Blevenec had stored his cider. The gendarmes crouched to enter. They felt along the walls and shined a flashlight in the dark corners. "I feel something. Over here!" shouted one of them. Anxiously they dragged out a wooden crate. But once in the light, it proved only to be a crumbling box with rusted parts of a cider mill that Monsieur Blevenec had left behind.

"We've found guns, explosives, and pamphlets about the illegal French rule of Brittany in farms all around the region," said one of the gendarmes.

"With instructions how to fight for independence," the other one added. "He must have been checking the layout here but didn't have time to store anything yet. His girlfriend was part of the movement, too."

"He told me France would be liberated one day. That's when I knew he'd been a collaborator. I didn't dream he was still actively trying to . . ."

They brought out small black professional-looking notebooks and jotted down their findings—or lack of them—for an official report to the chief of police in Rennes. Finally, after all these years, they had a crime to investigate. And what's more, La Salle was part of the crime!

⌒

The shock of David's betrayal consumed all my strength. After the house was back to normal, I had no energy left. It was as if someone had extinguished the light inside me; I felt nothing but emptiness. When I left Yves, I poured my sadness into my work. But now, for the first time in my life, I

had no desire to paint. Every day for a month, after dropping Danielle at school, I drove to Vannes and continued on
to *la côte sauvage,* the wild coast along the Quiberon penin-
sula. I walked along cliffs that dropped precipitously to the
ocean and listened to the roar of the waves. When it was
time to drive back to pick up Danielle at school, I moved
mechanically, eager to return the following day when once
again I could do nothing except watch the surf crash against
the rocks.

Stretched out on a cliff high over the ocean and in spite
of my efforts to empty my mind and think of nothing, I
asked myself how I might have handled things differently.
What if I had sent Mosca away—and not David? I didn't
blame him entirely; Mosca, sensing his weakness, had sub-
jugated him like the predator she was. But what good would
it have done? He was under her spell and surely would have
followed her. Thoughts came and wounded me like bee
stings and then evaporated like gusts of wind. Day after day,
I returned to the *côte sauvage* and watched the waves beating relentlessly against the coastline.

One afternoon, while meditating on my preferred perch,
a voice from the depths of my own consciousness invaded
my reverie. Hard as I tried to squelch it, the voice rumbled in
unison with the roar of the waves, taunting me with questions I had evaded so long: Wasn't it your failure too? Don't
you share the blame for the marriage falling apart? Think
back to the turning point. The moment that changed everything. The day he told you to stop painting. Remember? You
said nothing. You acquiesced. You exposed your weakness.
That was the very moment you opened the door to all the
endless, unreasonable demands that followed. But what if

you had refused? What if you had slammed the door shut, had been courageous and taken a stand at that critical moment and had declared, "I will never stop painting. Accept me and love me for who I am and what I am or leave me. Scream at me, pound on the table, but I will always paint. Not secretly, but openly and passionately, shouting to the world that I am a painter." Would he have left you? If you had, from the start, fearlessly set boundaries as to what he could or could not ask of you then or in the future, would he have realized the power of your strength and determination? Would everything have been different? Would you still be together, on equal terms, supportive of each other's needs and aspirations? Would he have dared to strike you? By bowing to his outrageous demands, didn't you plant the seeds of violence and heartbreak that were to come? The voice roared on, relentless. More accusations. More questions to which I would never know the answers.

Mosca left David soon after the confrontation. I saw him a few times after that. Our chance meetings were awkward and brief, and we never spoke of what had happened. Still, I never believed he would have allowed arms to be stored at La Salle, no matter how much he had been bedeviled by Mosca. After a while, we heard he went back to Scotland, and we never saw him again.

Danielle was bereft. The twofold trauma of the death of Pierrot and David's departure left her inconsolable. When she misbehaved, I scolded her and then it was forgotten. How could she understand that I had to send David away?

Even more troubling, it was the second time she had lost someone who was central to her life.

"She thought of him as a big brother," I said to Jeanne. "Whether he was right or wrong, she looked up to him. She misses her father terribly. Now David is gone, and not even Pierrot is here to console her."

"You couldn't let David stay on, not after what he did. It wouldn't be right, Mitch," Jeanne said. "The little one—someday, when she's older, she'll understand."

"Yes, in time. But what about now?"

"You can't keep her from pain, *ma fille,* any more than you can keep one season from giving way to the next. It has to be. *Elle va connaître la misère dans la vie.*"

There it was again. That phrase! She'll know life's misery. My beloved Jeanne, so full of life and resilient, yet even she repeats the Breton mantra that makes me shudder each time I hear it.

"Why, Jeanne? Why does she have to? She's so young. If she must, can't she wait until she's older to know *la misère?*"

Her wizened face assumed the look of a sphinx, as it sometimes did, as if her wisdom had been gleaned from centuries past. I watched her round, wrinkled face become unreadable and remembered how at two, she was sent to the fields to guard cows that towered above her. How terrified she must have been. She had no choice; she stayed and did as she was told. I thought of her as a small child, and the mounting responsibilities she had with the birth of each new sibling, and the overwhelming grief and fear she felt when her mother died. I thought of the solitude she endured when Luc was taken prisoner, and again when he died and she was alone on the farm with two young sons no older than Danielle. I thought of the sadness she must have felt all those years with Thérèse down the road who excluded her and who was jealous of her closeness with Claudine. I thought of long, cold winters without heat or running water in the house, the endless hours working in the stable and in the fields. I thought of her working all her life harder than I ever dreamed a woman had to do. How had she survived? How had she maintained her humor and thirst for life? Were some people born to withstand grief and adversity and remain full of life and optimism while others were destroyed by infinitely less?

Perhaps there was wisdom in expecting misery to be a part of life, in accepting the fact that we can't evade it. Trying to deny it only makes it more devastating, more lethal, so that when something tragic happens, we are unprepared and cut down by it. If that was so, then *tu vas connaître la misère* wasn't pessimistic; it was an ancient way of looking at life, an acceptance of whatever may happen. The good is tempered by the knowledge that it is a part of life. Expecting misfortune mitigates the inevitable return of sadness. The good and the bad are not opposites, but rather intertwined and inseparable parts of the whole. *Tu vas connaître la misère dans la vie* no longer sounded like a threat. As sun-parched fields would become rain soaked, and then dry again, life too would swing from one pole to another. Life would be full and joyful one moment and stunned by loss and disappointment the next. Both were indispensable parts of the plan, as Jeanne said, just as one season follows another.

One day walking along the cliffs I regretted I didn't have my sketchbook with me. The next day, I began to paint again.

25

The Coif

"I KNEW YOU WOULD LEAVE ONE DAY."

"How did you know?"

"You weren't born on a farm, Mitch. Some people who are born on one can't handle it. It's not a life for everyone."

"Did you ever think of leaving the farm?"

"Me? *Dame*, no. It's all I ever knew, so crazy ideas never buzzed around in my head. Young folks today, like Jacqueline, maybe even Claudine, they could never stay on a farm. Once a girl knows there are other ways to live, all she dreams about is leaving. If she can't, she's miserable all her life, like poor Thérèse all these years. You grew up in a city, *ma fille*. How could you stay on a farm? Besides, a woman alone—without a man around to help? For a while, maybe. But not for long. It's too hard."

I went to her stove, brought the pot to the table, and poured coffee in our cups. "I've been telling myself there are other reasons," I said, "such as Danielle needing a better school, that she needs to be with children her own age to learn the kinds of math and science that Noël can't teach in a country school. That I have to make money, and that everyone in the Morbihan who will ever buy one of my paintings has bought one or two. It's all true. But you're right. I wasn't born on a farm. I love it here. I don't want to sell La Salle. I don't want to leave. Most of all, I don't want to leave you. But I have to. It's too hard for me."

"Where will you and Danielle go?"

"I thought of going back to Paris. But Yves is there, and the art world is small. After I sell La Salle, we'll have enough money to go to Rome. It's in Italy."

"Italy? They speak their own patois there, don't they?"

"They speak Italian."

"Can you speak it?"

"Jeanne, *ma chérie*. You know the answer to that question. But I'll learn."

She shook her head. "I suppose you don't know anyone there."

"You're right. But I can show my paintings in galleries. And there's a good French school in Rome for Danielle. Italy isn't far. I'll always come back to you. It won't be the same as living across the road from each other. But it's only a two-day drive or an overnight train ride. You know me; I'm a rabbit. I'll come back often."

A month later, she helped me pack.

⁓

Our last year at La Salle was bittersweet. I knew soon after David left I wouldn't be able to stay. Perhaps I had come to lean on him too much. Perhaps it was the shock of his betrayal; but now that he was gone, I felt lost. Of course, Jeanne was there for me as she always had been, watching over me like a mother hen, although I was never aware of it. I only knew that the moment I needed her, she materialized instantly and out of nowhere. That last year, we were closer than ever. Either I was at her house or she was at ours. I sold a few paintings and bought her the freezer I had wanted to give her for so long. It stood in the narrow hallway between her kitchen and the stable and was large enough for her to freeze a full harvest of fruits, all her vegetables, and a whole pig if she wanted to.

"Thank heavens," I said when I gave it to her. "You never once said, 'How much do I owe you?' Yves told me that everyone in the country had to say *'Combien je te dois?'* before accepting anything offered to them so they wouldn't feel obligated. I thought it was a terrible custom."

"We would have been saying that a lot, you and me. I hated the custom, too, but had to wait for you to come to the village before I could forget that nonsense."

Life without her—I couldn't imagine it. I wanted to emulate her, from the way she dealt with life's variants to the expression on her face when she whipped a batter of *quatre quarts*. I wanted to emulate how she made the best crepes, delighting Danielle and me by sending them soaring high in the air with an expert flip of her wrist and catching them in the pan on the way down without ever dropping one. I wanted to emulate how she grew the smoothest copper-colored shallots, and how she held one in her hand and rolled her thumb back and forth over it, feeling it, squeezing it, making sure it was firm to the core before picking it to cook with, or how she knew instinctively which herbs and grasses could cure an ailment, or the glint of mischief in her eyes that carried her through the worst of times no matter how bad things got. Like her mother, who jumped on a horse at full gallop, she leaped onto life, grabbing both reins and never slowing down. She was *disponible*; whenever an unannounced visitor came by, she would stop what she was doing, take glasses from her cupboard, wipe them with her apron, uncork a bottle of her best cider from the cave, and sit to chat, attentive, regardless of work waiting in the vegetable garden or in the field. To be present. To live each moment. Completely. Undividedly. I wondered how *disponible* I would be if one day I moved back to a city, with all its urban distractions.

Would I remember her? In time, would memories of her fade?

⁓

She was sixty-eight when I first saw her. Everyone called her Mémé. She had three cows to her name; she didn't know how to read or write and had never left her small village except on Sundays, when she expertly pinned on her crisp white lace coif of the Morbihan and walked three kilometers across the fields to attend Mass at the little country church in Sulniac. Until we met, she had never been in a car or spoken on a telephone.

The first time I took her to Vannes was on a market day when the sleepy town came alive at dawn. Farmers from miles and miles around poured in before sunrise to set up their stalls, and throughout the morning hours, people from nearby towns and villages converged to barter and socialize in tiny cafés that served stacks of crepes with homemade jams and galettes with ham and cheese, washed down with endless streams of amber-colored hard cider. By afternoon, a carnival atmosphere had overtaken and transformed the town. How she loved the crowds and excitement! Arm in arm, we let ourselves be swept along with the crowds, blending as if merging with shifting flocks of birds, first to an arcade crammed with pulsating, glistening, wriggling fish she had never seen before, each fisherman shouting over the din to grab our attention. Like a messenger heralding her arrival, her low starched white lace coif revealed her to be a Morbihanaise. Everyone greeted her; she struck up a conversation with everyone. At a vegetable stand, she chatted with the farmers, admired their colorful display and puzzled over a bushel of plump artichokes, which she had never seen before. Around a corner, we watched farmers selling and buying cows, goats, and turkeys caged like condemned prisoners in wooden crates. We saw chickens and rabbits, squawking futile protests and others just killed, explicitly displayed, their innards exposed, their lifeless heads dangling, their eyes fixing the moment of slaughter. "Disgusting!" I said, averting my eyes and pulling her away from the scene of crime.

By evening, the farmers had folded their stalls. The crowds and confusion evaporated as if an orchestra leader had held up a baton to signal "piano, piano . . . andante," and the town reverted to its usual languid pace. We walked along tranquil streets to the wharf to linger in an outdoor café that overlooked the harbor, sipping our cider. Tired but exhilarated, we watched the sunset burst forth, intensify to a feverish heat, explode with brilliant, fiery colors as if in reprise of the day's excitement, and then dissipate gently, silently over the harbor.

During that last year, Danielle and I took Jeanne to Versailles and to Paris. Everywhere we went, people on the street and in cafés recognized her coif and called out *"bonjour la Morbihanaise."* She smiled at them, joked with them, and was at ease wherever she went. The huge, immaculate gardens in Versailles with their graceful statues and luxuriant fountains thrilled her; she shook her head in disbelief and uttered an occasional "Merde, *alors!*" as we strolled through the gilded, gold-laden rooms of the palace. It must have seemed unreal to her. But she never tired and was always eager for more. After Versailles, we drove on to Paris. I had dreamed of taking her there for such a long time. When I first mentioned to her that Danielle and I had to go to Paris for a few days and I wanted to take her with us, she didn't say a word. But her face lit up and her eyes shone more brightly, and I knew she would come. I gave her a small suitcase to pack anything she might want to take with us. "Take with me? What sort of things, Mitch?" she asked, puzzled. In her whole life, she had never left her farm, except for a brief stay in the clinic arranged by Dr. Le Bec, so many years ago.

We checked into the little hotel on the Left Bank where I had stayed when I first arrived in Paris. I would never forget the expression on her face as we entered the tiny hotel lobby and signed in at the desk. It was that of a child seeing something she had never imagined and wondering if it was real. I thought she would be terrified of the rickety elevator that took us to the fourth floor, but she was too elated to be frightened. *"La boîte qui monte!"* She gasped incredulously. "The box that climbs" rattled to a shaky halt on the fourth floor, and we followed the footsteps of an underaged bellboy carrying our bags to our rooms. Danielle and I shared one room, and Jeanne had an adjoining one with a shared bathroom between us. It was the first indoor toilet she had ever had at her disposal, let alone a bathtub and bidet. When I finally persuaded her to leave the wonders of our rooms, we left the hotel to explore Paris. It was a perfect spring day to *strani*, to wander about, as she would say in Gallo, with the magical Parisian light filtering through clouds, softly illuminating the glorious city. Arm in arm, with Danielle skipping alongside us, we strolled next to the Seine, wandered across bridges, and meandered down winding streets packed with shops, restaurants, and cafés. She marveled at shop windows, parks, tree-lined boulevards, tall buildings, crowds of people, traffic jams, and subterranean métros. For me, showing Paris to her made the enchantment of the city come to life all over again.

We stopped in every café or pastry shop that tempted us, to rest and watch the city parade before us. In one café, the owner was from a nearby village in the Morbihan and immediately recognized her coif. He greeted Jeanne like a favored relative, and although they had never seen each other before, they exchanged the customary four kisses on both cheeks. Wherever we went, Jeanne delighted in everything new; every discovery served to whet her appetite with the obstinate exceptions of the telephone and the television. On these, she never relented. On the way to and from Paris, we avoided highways, drove along back roads, told stories, relived what we had seen on our trip, laughed, opened the windows wide, and stopped a thousand times along the way for picnics or if we spotted something we wanted to see more closely. After a while, she no longer looked upon my camionette as a death trap, although she maintained a visceral distrust of all the other cars on the road. Our lives could not have been more different. To every outward appearance, we had nothing in common. Yet I never felt as close to anyone. I wondered, would she miss me when I moved away, or would she be content to resume her life as it had been before I arrived at La Salle—the same repetitive, unchanging routine, season after season, day after day?

I did go back. The first time was in the fall, a few months after Danielle and I had settled in an apartment in Rome. The new owner who had purchased our half of La Salle was a woman writer from Paris. She said there were houses to spare and I could stay there whenever I came to visit. I slept in the old temporary house, David's house, and stayed for a week. It was as if I'd never been away. Jeanne and I had long visits. We told each other everything that had happened, not forgetting any detail, no matter how trivial nor how small. From Italy, I telephoned Roger a few times and urged him to bring her to the phone. She forced herself to talk into it, but her voice was shrill, and I could tell she was ill at ease and hated it. A year later, I went back again when Marcel died. I expected to find her in mourning, but she was the same as always. Over a glass of cider she said matter-of-factly, "Death comes sooner or later to all of us. Nothing we can do to change that, Mitch. Marcel and I had a good life together. He was a good man. A hard worker. That's all you can ask."

Months later I left Danielle with friends in Rome and went back again to La Salle. Jeanne had been in my thoughts constantly. A huge void ached inside me, and I wondered if I had made a terrible mistake, leaving the village and putting so much distance between us. Did I foresee it was the last time I would see her? I slept on a cot in her kitchen so we could spend every minute together. I found myself watching her intently as if I were trying to memorize every detail about her. I watched how the corners of her mouth turned upward when she began to smile, how her face crinkled, and how rays of light danced in her eyes. I wanted to remember the warmth of her smell, which reminded me of apples and cinnamon simmering on the stove, and how being near her was like being enveloped in a protective shell that made everything seem safe and right. In this small, simple kitchen, with its long wooden table and hard, backless benches, with its dirt floor and old, blackened iron pot suspended over lingering coals emitting aromas of cabbage soup, of all the places in the world, I had found the one sanctuary I had ever known—the one place of unconditional love, the one safe place to be myself. Watching her as she bustled around the fireplace and stove, I felt I was watching my mother as I remembered her when I was small, or how, as a child, I used to watch my grandmother putter around the kitchen. Sometimes it seemed I had stepped back in time so I might know her. I had left the present and was reliving a time that no longer existed, watching across the room an ancestor whom I had loved more than anyone, past, present, or future. Time spun backward and forward, as if out of control. It didn't matter. All that mattered was that moment, there, in that kitchen, with Jeanne.

One day, she brought out the old shoebox that contained her coifs. From the bottom of the box, she lifted a beautiful starched lace coif she had kept wrapped in tissue for well over half a century. It was the coif she had worn when she was sixteen, the one she was wearing in the wedding picture on the kitchen wall, when she married Luc Diquero. From the way she unwrapped it, I could tell how precious it was to her. She sat next to me on the wooden bench and slipped six straight pins through my hair to pin it on me. Then she went to the cupboard and brought out an old smoky hand mirror for me to see for myself.

"It becomes you," she said with a satisfied grin. "I want you to have it, *ma fille*."

"I'd love to have it. More than anything."

"It will bring you luck. It's for your wedding day."

"Jeanne, my darling. I don't want to disappoint you, but I can't imagine ever marrying again."

"You think that way now, but you'll change."

I smiled and then became serious. "I don't think so. I've learned to live with disappointment and sadness. But some wounds never heal."

"Listen, Mitch. My whole life I've spent around cows. I think like them by now. You've heard the wail of a cow when its calf is dragged off to market? A part of the cow has been stolen from her. It's like she's dying, pleading to be put out of her misery. And yet, two days later, she's back in the pasture, mooing and calm as can be."

"On the outside. But how do we know how she really feels?"

"No matter how much it hurts, *ma fille,* no matter how much the suffering, we've got to let go of pain."

"Resign ourselves to whatever happens in life? Be like cows and head back to pasture?"

Jeanne nodded. "You'll trust someone again. You'll marry again. And when you do, you'll wear the coif and you'll think of your Mémé."

26

Forget Me Not

For a long time, I had no news from La Salle. Until shortly before his death, Marcel wrote to me regularly. I cherished his letters. In the handwriting of a diligent schoolchild and spelled phonetically, they were warm and filled with news. After he died, Claudine wrote me from time to time. Then she married a handsome soccer player from Theix. After that, I didn't hear from her for a while. Finally I got a letter from her. She said Mémé was doing poorly. Then she changed the subject to news of La Salle. That was all.

The letter was postmarked a month earlier. But when had Claudine written the letter? And what if she hadn't mailed it right away? Meurice, the postman, stopped by villages only from time to time. What's more, the Italian postal system was notoriously slow. I read it again and again. "Mémé has been doing poorly." What did it mean? I was frantic. I telephoned Joseph Blevenec. He told me Jeanne Montrelay had died. *"When?"* I cried. Two weeks ago. I froze. I could hardly focus on his words. After I hung up, I vaguely remembered him saying that Jeanne had gotten sick, and with Marcel gone, living alone was difficult. Thérèse refused to care for her or take her in. When she could no longer manage on her own, she moved in with her younger son, Marcel, and his wife, the other Thérèse. I tried to compose myself. I phoned them. Thérèse answered.

"Oh yes, she died, Midge," she said matter-of-factly. "About two weeks ago. She got real sick at the end. She moved in with us, but it was bad. She couldn't work for her keep or anything."

"Was she in pain, Thérèse?"

"I suppose so. She was a burden."

I was heartsick. Oh, Jeanne! All alone at the end. Sick, in pain, and alone. *La vraie misère.*

I remember the day I first arrived in Paris. I was young then, only twenty-eight. I was idealistic, impractical, and oblivious to warning signs. How could I have known I would find myself living on an isolated farm, transplanted to a small village in a remote section of the Morbihan, a place far from cities or towns or, for that matter, far from anything I had ever known or imagined? There were times the solitude was too much for me to bear. Sometimes I would drive to Vannes to sit in a café just to brush against people. I didn't need to know them or speak to them. Just feeling their presence soothed the ache of loneliness. I had grown up in a city, worlds away. I never suspected that one day I would marry a Frenchman who would take me to an improbable place where I would have to chop wood to build fires, wield a machete to slash through thornbushes, and live among peasants who were more like my ancestors than my contemporaries. Had I known what I learned along the way, I might have been wiser and have done things differently. But looking back, I wouldn't change anything that led me to Jeanne Montrelay. My life is divided in two: before I knew her, and after. Before I met her, I didn't know that women like her existed. Before I knew her, I had no idea how hard a woman's life could be or how brave and resilient a woman had to be to survive. Or how someone so intertwined with nature and centuries past could show me the kind of love for which I had always yearned. How could I have known, until I married Yves, and by a strange twist of fate, became the chatelaine of La Salle?

Years later, when Danielle was in her mid-twenties, we went back to La Salle. She had grown tall and slim, and sometimes wore her long amber-colored hair drawn back into a bun the way Jeanne used to do. With both Jeanne and Marcel gone, there was an emptiness, a consuming sadness about coming back. But both Danielle and I felt viscerally attached to the Morbihan and longed to see the hamlet again. Along the road, an old peasant woman, dressed in black and bent over, looked up and waved. I smiled and waved back and felt I would burst into tears. At the bottom of the hill, no one was home at La Sallette.

We drove up the hill and turned left into the courtyard. La Salle had been sold several times and now belonged to a wealthy family from the north of France who had restored and modernized the buildings to spend their summers there. At first, it seemed as if nothing had changed. The two sculpted wooden posts of Yves and me still stood guard at the entrance. The passage of time and frequent battering of storms had smoothed over the gash on my face and had aged the posts so that now they looked like ancient statues that had stood there forever. The light was the same as we remembered it; the early morning mist had cleared to make way for the sun, and we could see a glimmer of light on the gulf at the horizon, the way it had shone the day the old depository was torn down. No one was home. We crossed the road. Jeanne and Marcel's house was boarded up. We walked along the path to Thérèse and Roger's house; only a mongrel dog yapped at our heels to acknowledge our arrival. Everyone must have been in the fields.

We drove to the cemetery where Jeanne and Marcel were buried. It was a small cemetery on a hill overlooking fields and meadows, silent and peaceful. We searched for their graves up and down alleys lined with simple tombstones and ornate vases with plastic flowers. Danielle called to me from the end of one of the rows. She had found their two small inscribed tombstones.

⌐⌐

MARCEL MONTRELAY
bien aimé époux de Jeanne
1900–1983
JEANNE DIQUERO MONTRELAY
Mémé
1897–1987

⌐⌐

We placed an earthen pot of deep blue-violet hydrangea blossoms we had brought with us between the tombstones

(Jeanne would have liked that), and I sank down on the mound of earth over her grave. Danielle kissed me on the forehead and left to wait for me in the car so that I could be alone with Jeanne.

I stayed there for a long time. Tears filled my eyes. "She was a burden," Thérèse had said. I could hear her voice and imagine how brusque and impatient she must have been with Jeanne when she was weak, in pain, and could no longer earn her keep. I had always heard that old people in the country had to help out as long as they lived. But what about when they were sick, dying, and could no longer do their part? Were they to be discarded? Cast away? My darling Jeanne. No one had written me you were dying, but I should have known. Just as you knew each time I needed you at La Salle and you miraculously appeared out of nowhere. Why wasn't I with you at the end? Why I wasn't by your side to take care of you as I had done when Moomoot kicked you, and you had fallen against the stable wall? Why wasn't I with you to tell you I loved you and would always remember you? Why wasn't I there to talk to you, hold you, and comfort you when you were in pain? When you knew you were near death? Did you ask yourself why I didn't come? Did you feel I had abandoned you when you needed me most? Did you forgive me? Could I ever forgive myself?

Probably not. My tears were for her, for Marcel, and for the village, too. And I wept for myself. A way of life I had come to cherish and that seemed eternal had been swept away by modern times and existed no more. Jeanne had taken all that with her. Still, it was comforting to see Marcel's tombstone next to hers. They were together again. She wasn't alone anymore. I wiped my tears. Perhaps one day the ache of regret I felt in my heart would subside, and I would remind myself with wonder how many lives she had graced, an old peasant woman dressed in black who for nearly all of her life had never left her village. I leaned over her grave, pressed my cheek to the mound of earth, and whispered, *"Kenavo."*

Epilogue

⌒

DECADES HAVE PASSED SINCE DANIELLE and I moved to Rome and then returned to America. Long ago, needing to know the father who had disappeared so early from her life, Danielle moved back to Paris. In time, she found a way to be close to him. But would she ever find a way to ease the pain she had endured when she was very young and unable to understand? Would she ever fill the void gouged out by his absence? Perhaps not. But she would go on searching.

I am much older now. I am older than Jeanne was when I first arrived at La Salle. In spite of difficult times in the early years, I never stopped painting. After a while, I began to have exhibitions that were well received and enjoyed a certain success. Eventually I settled in Manhattan, a city as far removed from an ancient country hamlet as one could find. And yet, deep inside, there is a part of me that never left La Salle, that still takes lonely walks in Central Park almost as if it were a pine forest of years ago, a part of me that still presses my hands against the bark of a tree to imbibe its life force. Most of all, the memory of Jeanne Montrelay throughout the years has remained constant and alive. Rarely a day goes by that I don't feel her standing by my side, dressed in black, her gray eyes shining, the corners of her mouth drawing up into a smile, deepening the wrinkles on her face.

For many years I had thought of writing about Jeanne, but I was unsure how to go about it. Maybe a children's book, I thought. Or a portrait of her, in words. I never got around to it. I was too busy. Eight years ago, I underwent spinal surgery. Upon my return from the hospital, I was unable to walk, paint, or lift a canvas. I was in constant pain. Unable to do anything else, I began to write about her. Curiously, as soon as I began writing, the pain stopped—and as soon as I stopped writing, the pain returned. At first, I was suspicious. It must have been coincidental, I thought. But after several experimental startings and stoppings, I realized that as long as I wrote about my beloved Jeanne, I had no pain. Obviously, I was highly motivated and threw myself into writing the story. In time, contrary to medical prognoses, I was able to walk and began painting again. Recently I had a large show of my paintings, which was more successful than ever. Jeanne had looked after me before. Once again, she had healed me.

That we would become inseparable, as I look back in time, still surprises me. We went everywhere together, from visiting nearby villages to walking along the beach. From Belle-Île to Paris and the gardens of Versailles. We told each other everything. I can still see her stoking the fire, bringing the pot of coffee to the table, and sitting across from me in her kitchen across the road. Sometimes the memory is so real I can smell the hydrangea blossoms wafting through the lace curtains in the kitchen window. Whenever something vaguely connected to those years stirs her image to my mind, I can feel her presence as palpably as if she were beside me, and the details of her face rush into focus and are as clearly defined as the day we first arrived at La Salle, when she was standing by the side of the road and I first saw her.

Acknowledgments

⌒

WITH GRATITUDE TO MY AGENT, Liv Blumer, for her belief in the book, for her enthusiasm, humor, and insight; and to her assistant, Divya Sawhney, who was the first to read the book and send it on its way. My grateful thanks to my editor, Lauren Marino; her associates, Hilary Terrell and Brianne Ramagosa; and the editorial team for their invaluable counsel and support.

With everlasting thanks to Bryan Chadwick; Giuliana Mammucari; Laura Raedle Beckley; Fred Andresen; Jacques Lainé; Kate Hurney-Braverman; Betsy Prioleau; Cynthia Brody; my niece Joan Reed; Kristina Gelardi; Stacey Berman; and so many others for their friendship, reassurance, and generous help along the way.

With special appreciation to my friend, Geoff Stoner, without whose encouragement and contribution from the very start, this book could not have been written.

With loving thoughts to my daughter, Danielle, with whom I shared this extraordinary time of my life, whose luminous presence sustained me through the difficult times, and who, when she was very young, was nourished, as I was, by the Morbihan and the people we knew there.

My abiding affection and gratitude to Claudine Diquero Rio, Roger Diquero, Madame and Monsieur Blevenec, Monique Blevenec Lohezic, and all the villagers who appear in this book, who opened my eyes to a different world, and who enriched my life.

And with my thanks to the one person who was the inspiration and reason for writing this book and to whom it is dedicated, Jeanne. Her guiding spirit has stayed with me for all these years, and I am indebted to her in more ways than I can ever express.